Understanding
the Psalms

Understanding
the Psalms

GEORGE APPLETON
formerly Anglican Archbishop in Jerusalem

MOWBRAY
LONDON & OXFORD

First published 1987
by A. R. Mowbray & Co. Ltd,
Saint Thomas House, Becket Street,
Oxford, OX1 1SJ

Typeset by Acorn Bookwork, Salisbury, Wiltshire
Printed in Great Britain by
Cox and Wyman Ltd., Reading

British Library Cataloguing in Publication Data

Appleton, George
    Understanding the Psalms.—(Mowbray's
popular Christian paperbacks)
    1. Bible. O.T. Psalms—Commentaries
    I. Title
    223'.206   BS1430.3

ISBN 0-264-66923-1

Contents

v

Abbreviations

ASB   The Alternative Service Book
BCP   Book of Common Prayer
RSV   Revised Standard Version
AV   Authorised Version

The Psalms are poetry so moving that I can hardly keep my voice steady in reading them.

A. E. Housman

May our dear Lord, who has given us the Psalter and the Our Father and taught us how to pray them, grant us also the spirit of grace and supplication, that we may with delight and resolute faith truly pray without ceasing, for thus it behoves us. He has commanded it and desires that we should. To Him be praise and honour and thanksgiving.

Martin Luther

Introduction

The Psalms will always be associated with David, though scholars tell us that most of them were not written by him, for many refer to the Temple which was not built in his lifetime and others refer to happenings that took place long after his time. We know that he was recruited to play on the harp, the small harp held in the crook of his arm, to calm the troubled spirit of Saul, the first king in Israel.

Before he was called to carry out this royal duty, we can picture him watching over his father's sheep in some shady valley in the heat of the day, and composing words to fit the tunes which his fingers played. The 23rd psalm will always be associated with him, and psalm 51 may well be an expression of his penitence, after sinning with Bathsheba and then trying to cover up his sin by contriving the death of her husband Uriah.

The Book of Psalms is a collection of five smaller collections. The first book contains 41 psalms, most of which are attributed to David in the headings of the Hebrew Psalter. The last verse of psalm 41 is a doxology, perhaps added by the final editor to mark the conclusion of this first collection: 'Blessed be the Lord God of Israel, from everlasting to everlasting. Amen. Amen'. The next three books are similarly concluded (72.18–19, 89.50, 106.46), and the whole psalter ends with the glorious gloria of psalm 150, with the peak of human praise in its last verse: 'Let everything that has breath praise the Lord; O praise the Lord'.

The second collection 42–72 also has psalms associated with David, and at the end has a note 'The prayers of David, the son of Jesse are ended'. A few psalms included in the other three collections may have the heading 'A psalm of David', 'A prayer of David' or 'For David', leading the reader to the conclusion that this most loved of all kings was not only the first singer of many psalms but also the inspiration of later singers adding to the growing Psalter, meditating on David's example or his troubles, or perhaps wanting the prestige of his name for their own efforts.

David is spoken of as the sweet Psalmist of Israel (2 Sam. 23.1) and his last words are evidence of his personal dedication and poetic inspiration:

The Spirit of the Lord speaks by me
    his word is upon my tongue.
The God of Israel has spoken,
    the Rock of Israel has said to me:
When one rules justly over men,
    ruling in the fear of God,
He dawns on them like the morning light,
    like the sun shining forth upon a cloudless morning,
    like rain that makes grass to sprout from the earth.

                                                    (23.2–4)

The Psalter is often described as 'the hymn book of the second Temple' or not so often 'the prayer book of the Second Temple'. We may note that a considerable number of psalms first composed in a personal vein are made suitable by a verse or two adapting them to corporate worship. This practice is followed in Christian worship by adding a *gloria* to every psalm in a context of trinitarian faith.

All who are familiar with the psalms will notice that the second part of each verse is a parallel or extension to the first, doubling the message. A good example of this is: 'Create in me a clean heart O God: and renew a right spirit within me' (51.10).

Although many of the psalms express a narrow nationalism, the fact that many psalmists speak of the feelings, fears, despairs and hopes of the human heart, gives their poems a relevance to people everywhere in all ages. There are psalms that sound a clear note of universalism: God is the king of the whole earth, Jerusalem is the centre from which a universal kingdom will spread, with all nations becoming subject to the divine Law. Psalm 100 calls to all people to be joyful in the Lord and serve him with gladness; psalm 67 prays for a blessing on all nations; psalm 84 pictures God making up his register of nations, with Zion the spiritual mother of all; psalm 117, the shortest in the Psalter, calls all nations to come and praise him for his universal loving kindness; and the last verse of the whole Book of Psalms calls to everything that has breath to praise the Lord.

Jesus and his twelve disciples must often have sung a psalm or several in their evening worship as they toured the little towns and villages of Galilee, sometimes sleeping rough under the stars and often welcomed into people's homes. It may be remembered that to form a synagogue needed at least ten founding members (cf. Zech. 8.23). Jesus presided over his travelling synagogue, blessing God at their frugal meals, and presiding at the sabbath evening ceremony when a blessing of God would be said over bread and wine and distributed to all present. The two disciples at Emmaus became convinced of the presence of the risen Lord when they sat round the supper table and heard his familiar voice blessing God before they began the meal.

The psalmists pour out their hearts to God, sometimes in joy and thanksgiving, and often in desperate need in difficult personal or national situations. They often feel that God is angry with them or has deserted them, but

3

they open out the emotions of their hearts to Him. They often pray against their enemies in vindictive retaliation for cruel oppression and crying injustices. I often seem to note that after such embittered imprecations, their prayers become less bitter, as if the poison of hatred is being lanced from their minds as the pus is lanced from a boil on the body. The writer of psalm 62, ascribed to David in the Hebrew Psalter, makes an earnest appeal in verse 8: 'Trust in Him at all times, O my people: pour out your hearts before Him, for God is our refuge'.

There is no clear belief in the psalms of a satisfying life after death, only the idea of a vague, shadowy existence, greatly inferior to the present life, in which God does not seem to operate, though one must not forget the faith of the writer of psalm 139 speaking of God's omnipresence: 'if I make my bed in the grave you are there also', and the implied promises of psalm 16.10: 'For you will not give me over to the power of death, nor suffer your faithful one to see the Pit. You will show me the path of life, in your presence is the fulness of joy and from your right hand flow delights for evermore'. With most of the psalmists the time had not come when the many martyrs for their faith were making survivors re-think their attitude to death. Yet we may say that there is a belief in an existence, poor and miserable though it may be. Well before the time of Jesus, the Pharisees came to believe in resurrection. Christians in their experience of the risen Christ have confirming evidence of the Easter fact both for themselves and for loved ones who have 'died', a faith and trust that inspires us to see in death a door of hope into the eternal world in which the living God lives and rules, with the unfailing purpose of sharing that divine life with all his children in the here-and-now and to all eternity.

I have been very blessed and fortunate. As a boy of seven, I joined the choir of a village parish in Somerset in which my father was gardener to the local squire. There,

4

Sunday mornings and evenings, I learned to sing the psalms appointed for the day. When I was ten years old, the squire and my father and family moved to Maidenhead, and I duly joined the choir of St Luke's Church in which the choirboys sang evensong every day. My voice did not break until I was sixteen, so I got to know the psalms better. In theological college we, of course, said the daily offices, and after ordination I kept that discipline for the clergy. Ten years ago I came across Rabbi Cohen's commentary on the psalms, from which I learnt much of their background and meaning. I can never be thankful enough to Dr Cohen, whom I never met except in his invaluable book. I have been blessed too in being helped to meditate by godly priests and writers, and so be shown the relevance of each psalm to my own spiritual life and ministry, as if God was speaking directly to me.

The version of the psalms is that of the Alternative Service Book of the Church of England.

I hope that those who use this small book will meditate after the study of each psalm, relaxing the body, stilling the mind, and opening up their whole being to the incoming of the Holy Spirit, who leads us into deeper truth, growing love and holier lives.

Before I close this introduction, I must mention a most moving experience in my short time as a canon of St Paul's Cathedral when, at the close of the Sunday Eucharist, the choir sang psalm 150; the glory of the music and the majesty of the words lifted the heart to heaven and the presence of God.

The mention of this moment of rapt worship reminds me of the tribute of Richard William Church who was Dean of St Paul's from 1871–90:

The Psalms stand up like a pillar of fire and light in the history of the early world. They lift us at once into an atmosphere of religious thought which is the highest that man has ever reached. They come with all the characteristic affections and emotions of humanity, everything that is deepest, tenderest, most pathetic, most aspiring, along with all the plain realities of man's condition and destiny, into the presence of the living God.

George Appleton
Pentecost 1986

The Psalms

1   The two ways

This psalm serves as an introduction to the whole Psalter, contrasting the fate of the virtuous and the wicked. The Law of the Lord, the Torah, safeguards those who follow it; the way of the godless comes to nought.

Verses 1–4: The joyful way of the godly

5–7: The sad way of the ungodly

The Jerusalem Bible makes v.1 clear: 'How blessed is anyone who rejects the advice of the wicked and does not take a stand in the path that sinners tread, nor a seat in company with cynics, but who delights in the law of Yahweh and murmurs [reading meditatively] his law day and night'.

The godly man is like a tree growing near a stream, putting its roots deep down into the moist earth, so that the life-giving sap rises through the bark to every part of the tree.

The ungodly man is like a tree infected with elm disease, so that the bark is killed and the sap fails to reach branches, twigs, leaves and fruit.

In the end the psalmist tells us that the aim of the righteous succeeds and that of the wicked fails. A modern historian (Froude) says that history teaches only one lesson – that the world is built on moral foundations, and that in the long run things go well with the good and ill with evil men. We might feel that the key words are 'in the long run'. Trust in God and obedience to his will are needed.

Another psalm, 37, especially verses 1–10, emphasizes the same lesson, urges us not to fret about the present seeming prosperity of the wicked, but to wait patiently for God to vindicate those who trust in him. 'Let the Lord be your delight: and he will grant you your heart's desire.'

2   God's anointing

The background of this psalm is a time of international unrest, with hostile nations coming against Israel. The newly enthroned king is spoken of as a son of God, and in patriotic fervour is promised that 'the nations shall be his inheritance and the uttermost parts of the earth for his possession'.

In the 1662 version of the Psalms other nations are spoken of as heathen. In the ASB translation the term 'heathen' is used sparingly, following the Revised Version of 1884, which has the following paragraph in its preface: 'The Hebrew word *goyim* nations, which is applied to the nations of Canaan dispossessed by the Hebrews, and then also to the surrounding nations among whom the people of Israel were afterwards dispersed, acquired in later times a moral significance, which is represented in the Authorized Version by the rendering 'heathen' or 'Gentiles'. While recognizing the moral sense of the word, the Revisers have employed it much more sparingly than their predecessors had done.

The 1884 Revisers may have had in mind Acts 10.34, where Peter in the house of Cornelius says: 'Truly I perceive that God shows no partiality, but in every nation any one who fears him and does what is right is acceptable to him.'

8

Psalm 2 may be analysed in the following short sections:

Verses   1–3:   Hostile kings plan an attack
         4–6:   God derides their plot
         7–9:   The king speaks
      10–12: Warning not to rebel

The last verse strikes the same note as the opening verse of Psalm 1.

The occasion may be that described in 2 Sam. 5.17: 'When the Philistines heard that David had been anointed king over Israel, all the Philistines went in search of David.'

Verse 4 speaks of God as laughing Israel's enemies to scorn. This must surely be a case of creating God in man's image. God's laughter must be an expression of delight in creation and in godly actions, though we may perhaps think of God having a sad smile as he regards the foolishness and rebelliousness of people.

Verse 5 speaks of the divine authority given to the king at his crowning and enthronement on the holy hill of Zion.

Verse 8 may reflect the ritual practice of inscribing the names of national enemies on pots and then smashing them with iron rods to symbolize their destruction and defeat.

The closing verses seem to be wise advice to people in positions of responsibility: 'Be wise, be advised to think out your decisions with care, and carry out your duties with fear and reverence, and rejoice in so doing.'

This psalm was clearly one on which Jesus meditated, both in his baptism and in the 40 days' retreat that followed. In it his relationship to God as a loving and obedient son and his authorizing by the Father were revealed.

3   A morning prayer in danger

The heading of this psalm in the biblical versions describes it as a psalm of David when he fled from Absalom (2 Sam. 15 and 16). The first verse speaks of numerous enemies, the fourth verse of hiding on the holy mountain, while verse six suggests an army of enemies – indeed a Jewish translation, followed by Coverdale and the Book of Common Prayer, speaks of 10,000 against him.

The verses comprise four couplets of two verses in each:

1–2: His dangerous plight
3–4: God defends him as a shield
5–6: Complete feeling of confidence
7–8: Prayer for deliverance for himself and a blessing for all his people

Many feel that his cause is hopeless and that there is no help for him from God. Yet he believes that God has given him his royal dignity and will enable him to hold his head high again. He feels the sustaining power of God, and is able to sleep trustingly, and when he awakes he feels fortified to face whatever may come in the new day. So he prays for deliverance, knowing that his rescue comes from God and that the power of his enemies will be broken. Although many of his subjects have sided against him, he has no bitter feelings towards them, and ends with a prayer for God's blessing upon them.

We find in this psalm the first mention of the word *Selah* which occurs no less than 71 times in the Psalms. This is said to be a direction to the musicians and choir to have a little interlude of music at this point. For recital and meditation today, a pause for silent reflection would seem to be appropriate.

4 An evening prayer of trust

This psalm should be read with psalm 3. The writer feels that his trust in God in time of trouble has been vindicated, and a sense of tranquil joy possesses him. The choir master is advised, in the Hebrew version, that only string-music is to be the accompaniment.

Verse 1 appeals to God to answer his need as He has done when he was hard pressed before.

Verses 2–5 are an instruction to his enemies to cease their lying and opposition.

Verses 6–10 speak of his continued confidence in God.

Verse 3: The writer asserts that his kingship has been determined by God and is therefore confident that God will answer his call for help.

Verse 4: He urges his enemies to tremble before God and, in the quietness of the night, let their consciences speak and convince them of the error of their ways.

Verse 6: Times are hard and many are discontented and will turn to any leader who promises better things. This may refer to Absalom's rebellion.

Verse 7: David himself hopes for a better time, the light of God's countenance may smile upon them again.

He speaks of a feeling of joy in his heart, greater than people feel in a harvest of corn and wine and olive oil. His mind is at rest and he can sleep in peace, not kept awake by anxious fear.

5 Another morning prayer

The writer is in danger from treacherous foes, and before going to the Temple offers a prayer in which he prays that God who hates evil will not allow the wrong-doer to triumph.

Verses 1–3: He prays that God will hear his meditation as he looks up in trust, knowing that God is perfectly good.

Verses 4–5: He knows that God will not tolerate in his presence those who work mischief, speak lies, deal treacherously and shed blood.

Verses 6–7: As for himself, he comes to the Temple with reverence, conscious of God's great goodness and confident that God will lead him in a straight path.

Verses 8–10: His mind reverts again to the evil men, full of malice, with no idea of truth, whose flattering words lure others to downfall. He prays that they may fall into the pits that they have dug for others.

Verses 11–13: In contrast, the righteous who trust in God will shout for joy, assured that he will defend them, covering them with divine favour like a shield.

6   On the brink of death

The writer is still in the grip of a serious illness which has brought him near to death. He feels forsaken by God, punished in God's 'fierce displeasure'. In addition to his suffering of body and pain of mind, he is troubled by malicious ill-wishers. He is 'sore affrighted' and still in great pain, and wonders how long he can hold out. So he prays:

> Return, O Lord, deliver my soul;
> Save me for thy mercy's sake.

Like most of his fellow psalmists he thinks of death (Sheol) as a region beneath the world, where the spirit continues a shadowy existence, in which there is no remembrance of God even, let alone reasons for thanksgiving. Frightened by this prospect, groaning in his weariness, he weeps through the night. His sight fails, which suggests that he is an old man.

In verse 8 there is a marked change of feeling. His prayer has been heard. Perhaps the last three verses of the psalm were added later. In any case, his complaint is ended, there is joyful relief in his heart. Those who had previously mocked him are sent packing, overwhelmed with confusion, because they see that their taunts are baseless.

Those of us who live in the milieu of the New Testament know that God never forsakes sufferers or sinners; nothing can separate us from his love, his grace is sufficient for every situation.

7   Appeal to God as judge

This is another prayer against deadly enemies. The title in the Hebrew Psalter ascribes it to David concerning Cush the Benjamite whom the Talmud identifies with Saul. The psalm would well fit Saul's pursuit of David described in the later chapters of 1 Samuel.

Verses 1–2 pray for shelter against enemies as ferocious as attacking lions.

Verses 3–5 protest his innocence of any violence against friend or enemy. If he has done any such deed he is ready to be pursued and captured and overwhelmed with shame.

In verses 6–12, he appeals to God to declare him innocent and prays that the wickedness of the ungodly may cease. For God is the judge of all the nations and always condemns evil.

In verses 13–17, after picturing God coming out against evil doers like a well-armed warrior, he once again describes the plots of the wicked and the fate awaiting them. The mischief they have planned for others will recoil on their own heads; they themselves will fall into the pit they have dug for others.

In the last verse the writer thanks God for his justice, and states his resolve to sing praises to him as the Lord most High.

8 'Little less than divine'

The opening words of any psalm need more careful reflection than we are able to give them when we recite them in church or read them with the eyes in individual study. They are almost always words of faith and worship as well as of appeal. Mind and heart need to speak as well as voice. In this psalm the writer, followed by countless worshippers since they were first uttered, addresses God with the words 'O Lord our Governor'. There is no petition in it, no mention of any danger – all is worship.

This psalm is a meditation on the place of man in the universe, compared with the greatness of God and the vastness of creation. With our knowledge today of infinite space and endless galaxies of stars, countless light-years away, together with man's conception of exploring space, building, sending and manning rockets and bringing them back to earth, we can only gasp with wonder, yet find the writer's words still appropriate to our wonder, with a desire to enter into the mind of the Maker and be obedient to his eternal purpose.

The first three verses speak of the majesty of God acknowledged by angels in the spiritual sphere far out-reaching the created universe, silencing critics and all who oppose him. Yet that majesty is shown in 'the mouths of babes and sucklings', in the marvel of human speech and the ability to express thought. Parents greet with joy the first words of a baby and its ability not only to imitate the sound but to convey the meaning. There is perhaps the deeper thought that man is but a babe in the universe, a late-comer in developing creation, when compared with the age of the earth and the eternity of God. The Targum, which is the very early Aramaic translation of the Old Testament, words the phrase 'man became a living being' (Gen. 2.7) as 'man became a speaking spirit'.

In verses 4–5 the psalmist is conscious of man's physical insignificance, as he gazes at the light of the moon and stars as far as his eye can see. He asks himself 'what is man?' and then wonders why God should care for him or want to visit him.

Verses 6–9 speak of man's spiritual nature. God has made him only a little less than divine, endowing him with glory and honour, and delegating to him responsibility for the earth and its creatures (Gen. 1.28).

Verses 5–7 are quoted in Heb. 2.6–8, where the writer says that we do not yet see man fulfilling these high hopes but we see one who shared our nature for a little while and submitted to death, crowned with glory and honour, a pledge of the fulfilment of the promise of this psalm.

So man is called to great dignity but also to humble acceptance of God as Governor, who will direct him and hold him responsible.

In the light of such thoughts the psalmist repeats his opening words and pays a tribute of worship to God for his glorious revelation of himself.

9 Thanksgiving for victory

This psalm celebrates victory over national enemies, which may be the succession of victories of David, described in 2 Sam. 8, summarized in verse 14 of that account: 'And the Lord gave victory to David wherever he went'. God is described as 'Most High', that is over all kingdoms. He is the vindicator of righteousness and judge of all.

Verses 5–10 describe the completeness of the victory, which is evidence that God will judge the world in righteousness and deal justice to the nations (v.8). He is seen to be a strong tower to the oppressed, who will never forsake them that trust him.

The psalmist calls for praise to God for the great things he has done and for rescuing him from 'the gates of death'. He pictures the underworld as a walled-in area with gates. Hezekiah after his recovery spoke of his experience: 'I said, In the noontide of my days I must depart; I am consigned to the gates of Sheol for the rest of my years. I said, I shall not see the Lord in the land of the living; I shall look upon man no more among the inhabitants of the world' (Isa. 38.10–11). Jesus at Caesarea promised Peter that through faith the gates of death should not prevail against his church (Matt. 16.18).

So the writer, possibly David, says that he will give public thanks to God in Jerusalem, rejoicing in God's salvation, convinced that he is a judge of all the nations, who will assert his power and prove to them that they are but men.

10   Justice for the oppressed

In some of the ancient manuscripts this psalm and the one that precedes it are treated as one psalm. They certainly have the same theme of dependence upon God for rescue from evil men. In the previous psalm it was the victory over godless nations, in this psalm it is God's triumph over godless people within the psalmist's own nation. It seems to him that God is standing far off and hiding his face from his people in their trouble.

After this opening appeal to God for help, the psalmist in verses 3–12 describes the perverted thinking and evil actions of the wicked, who pursue their evil aims openly and even boast of it. They think that God is too far removed from the human scene to take notice of their doings.

In verses 13–17 the writer again appeals to God to come to the rescue of the poor and helpless, to break the power of the ungodly, and to search out and expose their wickedness until it exists no more.

The last three verses of the psalm are an expression of faith in the rule of God and his attention to their lawful desires, so that the poor and fatherless are given their right and need no longer be terrified by the godless.

11 Kept steadfast in danger

This is a psalm of trust in God when even friends may advise escape by flight, as a disturbed bird will fly away to the safety of hills or woods. The psalmist sees that law and justice, the foundation of human society, are being flouted and in danger of collapse.

The conditions described seem to fit the time when David lived in Saul's court and was subject to the king's obsession and hatred.

This short psalm falls easily into two parts: the first speaking of friends' advice that the writer should flee from danger (vv.1–3), and the second his confidence in God (vv.4–7). God scrutinizes all that is going on. He tries righteous and wicked alike. He approves the righteous and protects them but pours out punishment on the wicked.

The last sentence of this psalm says that 'the upright

shall see his face', meaning that the godly are admitted into his presence. Right living will draw the believer into closer contact with God.

12   Trust in God's protection

The psalmist feels that with so many enemies around him, it is difficult to believe that there is a single godly man left. There is widespread lying, flattery, double dealing and arrogance, and he wishes that God would wipe the wicked out (vv.1–5).

He hears God's answer in verse 6 promising what a number of psalmists call him to do: 'I will arise, and will set them in safety from those who snarl at them.'

Verses 6–8 show the psalmist's confidence in God's answer, knowing that the words of the Lord are completely reliable and pure, more so than purified silver and even more completely purified than the finest gold.

God will guard all who are attacked by these lying men, especially from those who surround him in the present. The psalmist is very aware of them and the way they strut around in pride and arrogance. He has not lost confidence in God, nor courage in himself, but he is conscious of wicked men everywhere and knows that many such men are in posts of authority. So the last verse implies another appeal for help.

13   Can God forget?

This little psalm is attributed to David in the Hebrew Psalter. That may be right, for the writer speaks of 'my enemy', who must surely be Saul when hotly pursuing

18

him and determined to kill him. In his long drawn-out flight he fears that God may have forgotten him and turned his face away from him. From the opening four verses, it would appear that he is in great danger and he fears that he may sleep the sleep of death. He prays that God will 'lighten my eyes', that is revive his spirit and restore his courage. Verses 1 and 2 speak of his trouble; verses 3 and 4 are his prayer; verses 5 and 6 express his relief.

It is as he prays that hope and courage are revived and his heart begins to rejoice in the assurance of God's salvation. So now he sings a song of joy, for now he has gained the victory over his despondence. Luther has an interesting comment on this psalm: 'Hope despairs and yet despair hopes', a result of trusting prayer.

14 A Godless world

This psalm could refer to the hard lot of Israel in a god-less world or to the righteous clement in the nation at a time of moral decadence. Both views may have been in the mind of the psalmist as he pictures God looking down from heaven on 'the children of men', the whole human race.

The opening word 'fool' means a vile person, an impious man rather than a philosophical atheist. In his heart he feels that he needs no religious faith, no moral standards, one who deliberately prefers evil to good. The psalmist with his own experience of God and his dependence upon God, feels that such a way of life is both wrong and foolish. God is irrelevant to such a man, as he is to many today.

The psalm may be divided into three clear parts: verses 1–4 describe the widespread corruption and verses 5–6 stress that god is with the righteous, cares for the poor, and will bring terror to the hearts of the wicked; verse 7, which may have been added later, makes the psalm relevant to the whole nation and appropriate for worship in the Temple. The writer longs for the time when Israel's fortunes shall be restored and God's sovereignty proclaimed to all the nations from Jerusalem. 'Then', he concludes, 'Israel shall be glad.'

Parts of this psalm are quoted in Rom. 3.10–12 where Paul surveys the moral condition of the world in his time, as pessimistically as the psalmist or Elijah at Mt Sinai (1 Kings 19.10).

Psalm 14 is repeated almost word for word in psalm 53. This may be due to an oversight of the collector and editor, or he may have felt that the message was so important that it could well bear repetition.

15 The good man

This psalm is second only in popularity to psalm 23. The Talmud, the authoritative collection of Jewish law, thought and tradition says that all the 613 commandments of the Pentateuch are summed up in this psalm. In it are set out the qualifications for entry into the divine presence, thus answering the question asked in its first verse: 'Lord who may abide in your tabernacle, or who may dwell upon your holy hill?', both understood figuratively.

It would be difficult to find a more concise and clear description of the character required of the one who has access to God and enjoys the relationship with him. He is uncorruptible, does always what is right, speaks the truth from his heart, never speaks a slanderous word, does no evil to his neighbour, he judges a man by his true character, gives no honour to worthless men but pays respect to Godfearing men, and never goes back on his word.

Verse 6 is interesting, particularly as this psalm is a favourite one for memorial services in the City of London: 'He has not put his money to usury.' This probably refers to lending money to a needy friend, rather than investing money in a joint commercial enterprise.

The second part of this verse is strongly emphasized in Judaism, the prohibition to take a bribe to corrupt justice and equally to accept a bribe.

The man who lives in this way will be able to withstand all the attacks and temptations of evil. More than that, he will be a welcome guest in the presence of the righteous and holy God.

16   Happiness in God

This is a psalm which shows the happiness that comes from obedience to God. The writer has found refuge in God in the past and prays that God continue to safeguard him in the future. The second verse acknowledges God as his highest good. The Revised Standard Version has 'I have no good beyond Thee', Moffatt 'My welfare rests on Thee alone', a Jewish translation 'I have no good, but in Thee', and the BCP, still familiar to many, has 'My goods are nothing unto Thee'.

In verses 3 and 4, he claims that he does not associate with evil men, nor delight in the idols and other gods that others run after. In the next two verses he asserts that his inheritance is God. He is pleased with this and wants nothing better, the cup in his hand is a cup of blessing. Verses 7 and 8 tell how God instructs and guides him, even in the quiet hours of the night, while in the day he keeps God always before him, so he feels secure. His heart is glad, his spirit rejoices and his body rests in safety.

The last two verses suggest belief in life after death but the psalmist's thought is of God protecting him in this life, saving him from premature death, showing him how to live, giving him the fulness of joy in the consciousness of the divine presence. All this happiness comes from communion with God.

In the New Testament this psalm is quoted by Peter in Acts 2.25−28 as being fulfilled in the resurrection of the Christ. It is also quoted by Paul in Acts 13.35, again in reference to the resurrection.

Christians recite this psalm conscious of the happiness spoken of by the psalmist, enhanced by their faith in Christ who has brought life and immortality to light through the Gospel (2 Tim. 1.10).

17   Prayer under attack

In this psalm an upright man appeals to God to come to his rescue and to vindicate his cause. He is pursued by a band of enemies who are determined to destroy him. It is headed 'A Prayer of David', and could quite well describe his danger when pursued by Saul (1 Sam. 23.24−26), though some scholars think the religious experience expressed is too mature for such an early date.

In verses 1−5, the writer pleads before God his innocence: he asks only for justice from God, the just Judge, who knows men's hearts as well as their actions. His steps have been firm in the paths of righteousness, the duties laid upon him by God.

In verses 6−9 he prays to be defended against the

attacks of enemies bent on killing him. He trusts in God as saviour and refuge, always steadfast in his love. Verse 9 combines two beautiful thoughts of God's protecting care: the 'apple' of the eye is the pupil, on whose soundness sight depends, and is therefore protected with great care; God also protects those who come to him as a mother-hen shelters her chicks under her wings, a metaphor that can be found in other psalms.

Verses 10–12 describe the enemies who surround him, pitiless and arrogant, watching for any opportunity to seize him, like a lion looking for a kill.

The next three verses are an appeal to God to act and destroy these ruthless enemies, while the final two verses are a prayer for the prosperity of the righteous. The psalm ends with the confident hope that those whose cause is just will be allowed to stand in God's presence and see God as he really is. The phrase 'when I awake' can be interpreted in different ways. It may mean 'when I awake from sleep every morning'; it could refer to awaking after a long night of danger and sorrow into the assurance of God's constant protection; it could refer to awaking after the night of death to the full vision of God in his eternal morn. In the light of our understanding of the New Testament it could include all three. 'When I awake and see You as You are I shall be satisfied.'

BCP has 'When I awake after thy likeness I shall be satisfied with it,' suggesting that it is only as we grow into the likeness of God that we shall be able to appreciate his greatness, his wonder and his unfailing love.

18   Gratitude for victory

This long psalm in thanksgiving for deliverance is almost identical with a psalm in 2 Sam. 22, where it is attributed to David 'when the Lord delivered him from the hand of all his enemies, and from the hand of Saul'. It opens with an expression of loving gratitude to God whom he describes as his strength, his rock, his fortress, his mighty saviour and deliverer, who has rescued him from all his enemies (vv.1–3).

Verses 4–21 describe the danger he was in and his narrow escape from death from which he was rescued by God's intervention, which is described in terms of an upheaval of nature – earthquake, dark storm clouds, thunder and lightning, of such a violence that laid bare the springs of the sea and the foundations of the earth. God is depicted as riding upon a cherub and swooping down in cyclones of wind, manifesting his anger against the persecutors of the righteous. In and through all this, God has upheld and rescued him, coming down to save him from the waters that threatened to overwhelm him.

All this was a reward for his righteous life and his trust in God which not only received God's approval but delighted God's heart. In verses 22–26 the psalmist speaks further of his faithfulness, his attention to God's laws and his blameless life, which God rewarded in this amazing liberation.

He goes on to speak of God's dealings with men generally, with those who are faithful he reveals the divine faithfulness, those who are pure experience him as supreme purity. But the crooked he is able to defeat and brings down the proud and arrogant.

In verses 30–31 he speaks of his personal experience of God in guiding him, giving him a lamp that makes his darkness bright, and strengthening him to put to flight a whole troop of enemies, and to leap over the wall of a city in which he may seem besieged.

God's way with the righteous is perfect: he defends them as with a great shield, he is a rock that cannot be shaken, he makes the psalmist's feet sure-footed and

24

swift, he trains him to resist adversaries, to bend a bow of brass and shoot arrows of steel, upholding him so that he does not fall or stumble (verses 32–38).

Verses 39–47 describe his success with God's help, putting enemies to flight, so that they finally submit and acknowledge him as the greatest king among the neighbouring nations.

In the last five verses the psalmist blesses God for his deliverance from violent attackers and for his victory over them, and pledges himself to ascribe the glory to God. The very last verse mentions God's faithfulness to David, his anointed, and expresses his confidence that God will continue this triumphant success to his successors, though this 'promise' may seem to be the addition of an editor, adapting the psalm for the worship of Israel in the Temple.

The Christian putting himself in the place of the man who wrote this psalm may wonder what message it has for him. Not many people today have so many ruthless enemies as the psalmist had. Our enemies today are much more psychological and spiritual – fears, anxieties, pressures, depressions, mishaps and misfortunes. God is still unchanging, still our refuge, the unshakeable rock on which we can safely stand, the refuge in which we can find safety, comfort and courage. He will still keep us warm and protected, as a mother-hen shelters her chicks. Each of us is the 'apple' of God's eye. His supporting grace will carry us through everything that happens. Like the psalmist, we can look back on all the difficulties of the past victoriously surmounted, we can love him in return for his love, and we can face the future with similar trust because of his unchanging goodness. And we can resolve, like the psalmist, to live in God's way, wanting to know and obey his wise and loving will, confident that that will bring peace of heart, happiness and blessing. Always there is his grace for every need, inexhaustible grace for anything that may happen.

19   Two powerful witnesses

A quotation from the philosopher Kant aptly sums up the message of this psalm for Christian readers. 'There are two things that fill my soul with holy reverence and ever-growing wonder — the spectacle of the starry sky that virtually annihilates us as physical beings, and the moral law which raises us to infinite dignity as intelligent agents.'

We who live on this earth in an age when astronomers tell us of new galaxies coming into being, extending into infinite space, and at the same time know something of the nuclear multiplication of energy, and are becoming aware of the depths, conscious, subconscious, unconscious levels of our interior life, together with something within ourselves that passes judgment both on acts committed in the past and planned for the future, are moved to even greater feelings of awe.

The psalm falls into three clear and distinct parts: verses 1–6 speak of the revelation of God in nature, particularly as we gaze at the vast expanse of the heavens by day and night; verses 7–9 tell of the revelation of God in the Torah, the divine Law with its insights, its directions for moral and holy living, its commandments both negative as to what is to be avoided and positive as to what is to be practised, the values by which men shall live; the concluding three verses are a prayer that the writer may be cleansed from every kind of sin, those that we are not even aware of, as well as those of a more deliberate nature.

The Hebrew psalter attributes this psalm to David,

though scholars think that the first section may go back to him, in which the name God denotes the God of Creation, while in the second part 'the Lord' suggests the God of covenant and grace. Also, this psalm is related to Psalm 119, the great exposition of the Torah, the divine Law, thought to be of a much later date after the exile. To the worshipper today, meditating on its relevance to his own life, it seems to have a satisfying and beautiful unity.

The revelation of God in nature is illustrated from the sky and the sun. As day follows day there is a silent communication of continuity. The psalmist sees the same continuity at night, with one night, as it were, passing on its witness in silence. As we gaze at the myriads of stars at night, we are one with Abraham as he stood outside his Bedouin tent and gazed in wonder at the endless heavens, or with Mohammad 2500 years later as he gazed at the same spectacle from his similar tent or convenient cave, and heard Allah speak.

The Hebrew poet thinks of the sun as a resplendent living being coming out each day from the dwelling place provided by God and passing over the whole earth each day, giving out its warmth, or like a bridegroom coming out of his chamber, the symbol of manly strength and human happiness.

In verses 7–11, the psalmist praises the Law of the Lord, using a series of names and attributes later expanded by the writer of Psalm 119 – it is true, it makes simple people who are easily led astray wise, it is perfect and right, its perception makes the heart glad, it is unchanging and endures for ever, though we must admit that our understanding of it becomes deeper and more clearly relevant to our changing lives and conditions as we journey through life.

The psalmist goes on to compare God's Law with the preciousness of the finest gold and the sweetness of

27

honey dripping fresh from the honeycomb. Moreover, he says, he is progressively taught and enlightened, and he knows that true happiness follows from obedience to all God's moral laws.

He then turns from his contemplation of God's glory in nature and his activity in the human heart to his own self, falling far short of God's glory and requirements, in secret sins which he himself does not yet recognize, as well as deliberate sins and sinful habits which need to be broken. He prays for cleansing and asks that his motives, his acts and his words may become acceptable to God. His last words are words of faith, worship and dedication: 'O Lord my strength and my redeemer'.

20 Prayer before a critical battle

This psalm is a prayer for the king as he goes out to fight a critical battle. It could well be a prayer for David on some such occasion. The community in Jerusalem prays for a royal victory as the king and his troops leave the city. The assembled people pray for his safety knowing that he will need divine help. They plead with God to remember his past worship in the Temple and the pious sacrifices that he has offered. They themselves hope to rejoice in his victory when he returns triumphant, with his prayers answered (vv.1–5).

In verse 6, the personal pronoun 'we' is changed to 'I', so it may have been sung by a single priest or cantor. It expresses confidence in God's help, symbolized by 'the victorious strength of God's right hand'.

The people answer, saying that their trust is in 'the Lord our God', rather than in the chariots and horses which the enemy may have in greater numbers. So great is their reliance on God that they believe that their prayers are already being answered, even before the battle commences. It is as if the battle is won already.

The last verse of this short national psalm returns to direct prayer: 'O Lord, save the king: and hear us when we call upon You', which is used as a versicle and response in the morning and evening services of BCP. In the ASB version the response prays for wisdom for the monarch's ministers and advisers, reminding us of our duty to pray for them both in the day-to-day government of any country and in the crises that arise from time to time. This psalm is indeed suitable as a prayer for all magistrates and people in high office as Martin Luther urged, and for the Church—Kingdom of Christ as directed by John Calvin.

21 Thanksgiving after victory

This psalm may be taken as a sequel to Psalm 20; equally it could be interpreted as a thanksgiving for a long and successful reign. It has also been regarded by some as having a messianic relevance.

The first seven verses speak of God's blessings to the King – success, long life, happiness, a sense of God's presence with him and confidence for the future ('he shall never be moved').

Verses 8 – 12 are addressed to the king. ASB has 'your hand shall light upon your enemies', whereas Cohen's Hebrew Psalter has 'thy hand shall be equal to all your enemies'. But the sense of all the versions is that they must be utterly destroyed, burnt like fuel in a fiery furnace, hostility must be destructive of them and their seed, the king and his troops must be ready to meet their advances with a storm of well-aimed arrows. The king is expected to root out every trace of evil.

The final verse is a kind of doxology in which all present join in acknowledging God as the Lord of great strength, who will give victory again if Israel is attacked in the future.

22 A cry for help is answered

This psalm is a cry of perplexity and pain of one who feels that he is abandoned by God. Yet he still calls out 'My God! My God!' However much he feels that God has forsaken him, he does not forsake God. So he pours out his heart to God in despair in the first 22 verses.

Verses 1–8 describe his despair and the mocking of enemies. He feels that he is like a worm, trodden under foot, not treated as a human being. His long continued loneliness and suffering make others feel that his former professions of faith cannot have been sincere, otherwise God would have rescued him by this time. Yet in the depths he remembers how God delivered the fathers in Israel, and he still hangs on to his belief that God is holy and righteous. This section ends with the taunt 'He trusted in the Lord, let Him deliver him if He delights in him'. These mocking words only remind him of God's care since his birth. He compares his enemies to wild bulls and lions that roar and rend. He appeals to God 'O go not from me, for there is no one else to help'.

He goes on to describe his physical suffering, fevered and emaciated, his limbs hardly function, his bones stick out, and worst of all his heart is like melting wax, all courage and strength gone. Again he prays 'O Lord, do not stand far off: You are my helper, hasten to my aid' (v.20).

In the second half of the psalm (vv.23–32) there is a marked change of mood. The psalmist's prayer has been answered. His heart is full of gratitude and his voice, bursts into praise. He wants all his friends to know of what God has done for him and the whole congregation of Israel to hear his grateful thanksgiving. He invites the poor and humble to share in his sacrifice and blesses his guests 'May your hearts rejoice for ever' (v.27).

His thought and vision spread out further to all the nations, 'Let all the ends of the earth remember and turn to the Lord: and let all families of the nations worship before Him' (v.28).

His faith has not yet extended to those who have died, yet perhaps in verse 30 there is a note of regret and a hint of hope.

He concludes with the assurance that his children will know of God's blessing to him; a future generation, as yet unborn, shall learn of the Lord's goodness (vv.31–32).

Many commentators think that the writer of this psalm expresses his feelings as a member of the community of Israel at a time of national trouble and suffering. Yet one cannot help feeling that the whole psalm comes from the heart of one who has suffered deeply in his personal life. It may be that later readers saw in his sufferings a picture of the sufferings inflicted on Israel. In any case the psalmist's faith is vindicated and his prayer, whether for himself or the nation or for both, is gloriously answered.

The possibility that Jesus was meditating on the whole of this psalm and not just on verse 1 is considered in the short chapter entitled 'Jesus and the Psalms'.

23   Shepherd of souls

This is the best known and most loved psalm in the whole of the Psalter. A Christian writer (Davison), quoted with approval by a Jewish scholar, pays it this tribute: 'The meaning and helpfulness of this perfect little psalm can never be exhausted as long as men, like sheep, wander and need guidance, and so long as they learn to find it in God their Shepherd'.

In the Hebrew Psalter this sunny little psalm has the simple title 'A Psalm of David'. Indeed, it is not difficult to imagine that he is the author and this a song sung as he minded his father's sheep, strumming on the little harp in the crook of his arm.

In the heat of the day the shepherd leads his flock into shady pastures of tender grass near to quiet flowing streams where they may safely drink.

So the Lord refreshes each soul, as Jesus promised the weary and heavy-laden, and guides each in the right paths.

The original Hebrew of verse 4 speaks of walking through dark valleys and it was a later interpreter who related it to the darkest of all valleys, the shadowy valley of death. There are other valleys through which most of us have to pass at some time or another – the valley of depression, bereavement, even failure and disgrace. In all of them we need have no fear, for the shepherding Lord is with us. He carries a rod, a weapon of defence against wild animals or robbers and a staff on which to lean as he watches over his flock and occasionally to guide a wayward sheep.

'You spread a table before me in the face of those that trouble me' – inspecting the grass for poisonous snakes, or viewing the terrain for attacking men or animals.

'You anoint my head with oil', soothing any hurt from brambles and refreshing tired sheep with a brimming cup, as he counts them back into the fold in the evening.

As the psalmist thinks of the care of any good human shepherd, he is assured that the Shepherd of all will follow him all the days of life and, when life is ended, he will dwell in the eternal home of God.

24   Welcoming the worshippers

This psalm is thought by Jewish commentators to have been composed for the occasion when David brought the Ark from the house of Obed-edom to the tent in Jerusalem which he had prepared for it. (See 2 Sam. 6, and 1 Chron. 15.)

Verses 1–2: Although Zion is God's appointed place of presence, his sovereignty extends over the whole universe. This thought was expressed by Solomon at the dedication of the Temple: 'Behold, heaven and the heaven of heavens cannot contain Thee; how much less this house that I have built' (1 Kings 8.27). The whole world, all it contains, including the inhabitants, belongs to God (v.2). The world was thought of as resting upon subterranean waters (Gen. 7.11).

Verses 3–6: These show the moral character necessary for all who would enter: 'clean hands' – unstained by violence and dishonesty, 'a pure heart' – free from deceitfulness and wrong motives, 'who has not set his soul upon idols', reminiscent of the first four of the Ten Commandments, 'or sworn his oath to a lie' – echoing the ninth Commandment. Such a righteous man will receive God's blessing and salvation: 'them that seek Thy face' – who discipline themselves to be worthy of entry into the divine presence. The worshipper cannot but recognize his own unworthiness and falling short of God's glory.

Verses 7–10: The entrance of the Ark through the gates into the city: 'lift up your heads' – the gates are thought of as too low for the majesty of God. In verse 8, the waiting priests are thought of as challenging those about to enter: 'Who is the king of glory?' The answer of the procession is 'The Lord of hosts, the Lord mighty in battle' who has given David victory over the Jebusites. The question and answer are repeated in verse 10 to emphasize its meaning and importance. 'The Lord of hosts' may mean 'the Lord of victorious armies'; it may also mean 'Lord of the heavenly hosts', as in the vision in 1 Kings 22.19. In this second meaning faith in God as Supreme Ruler of the universe echoes verse 1.

This psalm was traditionally sung in the Temple on the first day of the week. In Christian worship it is sung or said monthly and often chosen for the dedication of a church and for subsequent annual commemoration.

Further meditation is provided in Psalm 132 where the psalmist speaks of the intention of David to find a worthy resting place for the Ark, the symbol of God's abiding presence.

25 The prayer of a humble soul

This psalm, which is in the form of an alphabetical acrostic in the Hebrew psalter, makes clear that the writer was a prayerful and humble soul, relying on God's protection, eager to be taught by God and to receive guidance for his life. Its heading is 'A Psalm of David', but its final verse suggests that it may have been written during the troubles of the exile, though that verse might have been added by a later editor to adapt the very personal prayer for liturgical use for the community of Israel.

Verses 1–7 are an appeal for protection, guidance and pardon, and verse 3 expresses the aim of the whole psalm: 'Shew me your ways O Lord: and teach me your paths'. He remembers God's compassion and loving kindness in the past, and asks for God's mercy for the sins of his youth which evidently still trouble his conscience. Every day he raises his soul to God in hope, calling him 'the God of my salvation'.

Verses 8–14 speak of God's goodness to the humble

soul who remembers the covenant of Sinai and tries to obey God's commandments. He is confident that when he does so his heart is at peace and his children will live in prosperity. He knows that an intimate relationship with God will bring understanding of the meaning of life.

Verses 15–21 show that he still has enemies who hate him, that often he feels alone in anxieties and troubles. He comes to God for refuge, protection and forgiveness, praying that his present innocence and integrity may be his guard.

Finally, in verse 22, he prays that the community of Israel may have the protection and deliverance which he has prayed for himself.

26   In the face of evil

This is the prayer of one who was often in the Temple which he clearly regarded as the place where God's presence was experienced and his glory manifested. He may even have been a priest, for he speaks of being 'about your altar', and he is conscious of the need for innocence in life, and of the duty of telling others of the wonderful works of God.

In the first three verses he speaks of his readiness to be tested and his mind and heart examined, much in the spirit of Psalm 139.23–24: 'search me out O God, and know my heart: put me to the proof and know my thoughts'. He is confident that he will pass the test.

Verses 4–8 are a vindication of himself. He has had no part with deceivers and hypocrites; he hates the way the wicked gang up together. Verse 6 is the heart of this self-vindication: 'I wash my hands in innocence O Lord: that I may go about your altar', a verse often used today by the Christian priest as he prepares to celebrate the Eucharist, or takes part in the ceremonial washing of his fingers before he handles the bread and wine.

In verses 9–12, he resumes the prayer of the first three verses, dissociating himself from scandalous sinners and 'men of blood'. He resolves to continue a life of integrity and realizes that he will need God's rescue and grace to enable him to do so.

The result of the psalmist's prayer is that he feels on safe ground, he can worship aright in the corporate services of the Temple.

27   Complete trust in God

Rabbi Cohen in his commentary on the Psalms has this memorable comment on its opening words, 'The Lord is my light': 'He illumines my understanding, cheers my outlook, and floods my troubled life with brightness.' The heading in the Hebrew Psalter is 'Of David', and the psalm could well be a prayer of David before his anointing, when pursued by Saul.

In verses 1–3 the writer expresses his trust in God as the stronghold of his life, so he need not be afraid even if a whole army comes against him.

Verses 4–6 speak of God as his refuge: his supreme desire, above everything else is 'to dwell in the house of the Lord' always, a phrase to be taken figuratively, meaning to be always conscious of God's presence with him and therefore safe from and in every danger. In that presence he will be aware of the beauty of the Lord and his sole aim will be to discover the divine will.

In verses 7–15 his thoughts are on the threatening danger and he seems to fear that God may desert him, but he still appeals to 'the God of my salvation', confident that though his father and mother may conceivably forsake him, the Lord will never do so. In verse 10 he urges himself to seek God's face and answers with the resolve 'Your face, Lord, I will seek' meaning 'I will always come to you, looking up to you for welcome and encouragement'.

The last two verses express his belief that his life will be saved and that he will enjoy the goodness of the Lord 'in the land of the living', and so be saved from the shadowy half-existence of Sheol, the underworld of the grave. In the last verse he addresses himself again: 'O wait for the Lord, stand firm and He will strengthen your heart', repeating his instruction 'wait I say for the Lord'.

This psalm is a good one for the believer to use today. When trouble comes, the heart is faint with fear, and the will needs bracing to continue to look to God for protection and courage.

28 Prayer in a crisis and thanksgiving after

This psalm is headed like the previous one, 'Of David', and opens with an expression of faith – 'O Lord my Rock'. He is in deep trouble and fears that if God does not answer him, he will be as though dead. So he lifts up his hands in prayer to God for help to the inmost and holiest part of God's dwelling place, comparable perhaps to the Holy of Holies in the Temple, in which case it would be later than David (vv.1–2).

He then prays that his fate may not be to perish with the wicked, who will receive their deserts for the evil in their hearts, for their refusal to heed God's warnings and for their wicked deeds. The psalmist is not praying against personal enemies but against evil doers, convinced that God will not allow them to prosper (vv.3–5).

The next two verses make it clear that his prayer has been heard and he praises God in song, while his heart dances for joy.

He then turns from himself to the nation, confident that God will make them and their anointed king strong, blessing them as his own people, guarding and supporting them as their shepherd for ever.

29   God speaks in the storm

This psalm is a graphic description of a storm, with flooding waters, reverberating thunder, gale-force winds breaking over the great cedar trees of Lebanon, reminiscent of the giving of the Law on Mount Sinai in Exodus 19.16–19, all symbolic of the majesty of God.

In the first two verses the 'sons of heaven', presumably the angels, are called to give due honour to God and worship him, conscious of the beauty of his holiness. We are reminded of the opening chapter of the Book of Job; 'Now there was a day when the sons of God came to present themselves before the Lord' and the first verse of the last psalm in the Psalter 'O praise God in his sanctuary, praise him in the firmament of his power', remembering too the more familiar words of the BCP 'O praise God in his holiness'.

In verses 3–8 we have the seven-fold sound of the voice of God, sometimes spoken of as the seven voices of God, successive peals of power and glory, claps of thunder coming on the mountainous waves of the sea, forked lightning, storms of wind shaking the mountains, the most stable items in nature, breaking the cedars of Lebanon the greatest and most firmly rooted of all trees.

Sirion, the Sidonian name for Mount Hermon, seems to skip like a wild ox, the hurricane of wind whirls the desert sands into blinding clouds, the forests are stripped bare. The angels, called upon to witness this terrifying spectacle, all exclaim 'Glory' in wonder and praise.

In verses 9–10 the storm seems to have subsided, with God pictured as calmly enthroned above the water-floods, reigning in majesty forever, promising strength to his people and blessing them with peace. It is interesting that after the theophany in storm, the conclusion is the divine gift of peace.

The believer in God will hear him speaking in the storms that arise in human life, both external and interior, and the Christian will remember Christ in a storm on the lake of Galilee when he spoke both to the storm and to the fearful disciples 'Peace! Be still!' In every storm, if we listen, we shall hear his voice in the heart and know that he speaks for the Father.

30   A never silent heart

The heading of this very personal psalm is 'A Song at the Dedication of the House' and it is ascribed to David. The question arises in the mind of the reader – 'which House?' It might have been David's own house, built before he decided that the Temple should be built as God's House, a place for the worship of God and a symbol of God's presence with his people. It is a thanks-giving for God's mercy after a time of distress, vividly remembered, possibly recovery from a serious illness which brought the writer near to death. Later it was given a national interpretation and possibly used at the dedication of the restored Temple after the exile, and later at the re-dedication by the Maccabees after its desecration by Antiochus Epiphanes in the second century BC.

Verses 1–5 are a thanksgiving for recovery from the danger of death which the writer thinks of as 'a land of silence' and as a dark hopeless pit, a disastrous end to life on the earth. He cries out to God to save him from this and now gives thanks that God has answered his prayer. As a result of this experience he learns something that will guide and comfort him for the future: 'heaviness may endure for a night, but joy comes in the morning', words that have become unforgettable in our English language.

In verses 6–10 he looks back on happy prosperous days when he faced the future with a feeling of self-confidence. Then came this serious illness when he feared that God had hidden his face from him, as many people still fear today. He remembers how in his dismay he had the faith and sense to call out to God for help.

Verses 11–12 tell how God answered his agonized prayer and his heart overflowed with joy. He resolves that in future he will never be silent in his praise of God: 'O Lord my God, I will give you thanks for ever.'

The Christian as he reads, hears and then meditates on this psalm, will pause at the original writer's despairing question 'Can the dust give you thanks or declare your faithfulness?' After a little reflection he will remember the risen Christ and answer the psalmist's question with a grateful and emphatic 'Yes!'

31   Faith under persecution

This psalm is the prayer of one who tries to live a righteous life and has been cruelly persecuted in the past, as he describes in some detail in verses 9–20. It looks as if he is now undergoing another bout of cruel treatment. So he cries out to God for safe shelter remembering God's rescue in the past (vv.1–8). The first verse is identical with the opening verse of psalm 71. We find other psalmists making the same request 'never to be put to shame', as if that is more hurtful than the physical inflictions. We have to remember that in the psalmists' days, most people regarded suffering as God's punishment for sin, and when someone was in distress, people looked for some sin, obvious or hidden, to account for it. There were also plenty of people ready to mock at God's apparent failure to come to the rescue.

In the opening of his prayer the psalmist begs for immediate help and expresses his faith, sometimes warningly, in God as his refuge, fortress, high rock and stronghold and prays to be released from the net of intrigue and threat that he feels caught in. Verse 5 is used as a prayer in the late-night service of compline, with a significant change of tense, from 'you will redeem me' to 'you have redeemed me'. But it needs to be remembered that in the psalmist's time the prayer was to be saved in, and for, this present life. The last verse of this first section speaks of present rescue, so that he no longer feels hemmed in. BCP speaks of this somewhat quaintly as 'Thou hast set my feet in a large room'.

Verses 9–20 speak of his present plight, giving the impression of a previous experience of persecution. There are echoes of his complaint in Jeremiah 20.7–11 (or perhaps the prophet is echoing the words of the psalmist). Jeremiah concludes, with faith, that his persecutors will not overcome him, his enemies will not succeed in their plotting. No paraphrase can equal the translation of ASB which makes the psalmist's words come alight in modern terms for today, or of that in BCP, for those who still find it more satisfying to pray in Elizabethan English. Both translations are punctuated

41

by flashes of faith – 'have mercy on me O Lord', 'in You have I put my trust', 'You are my God', 'my days are in your hand', 'make your face to shine on [me] your servant'. The outpouring of soul concludes with prayer, typical of most of the Psalter, that the insulters may be put to shame, which perhaps an honest Christian may sometimes rightly pray, though not that they 'be brought to silence in the grave'.

In the final section (vv.21–27) the writer praises God again for his protection: 'O how plentiful is your goodness stored up for those who fear you', who shelter under God's covering presence. He admits that in his alarm he spoke hastily, afraid that he was cut off from God's care, yet pleading that he called to God for help. He exhorts all faithful believers to love the Lord and reminds them of the words which Joshua heard God saying to him, 'Be strong and of good courage'. So all can hope in the Lord.

Jesus clearly knew this psalm, for the first part of verse 5 was his last prayer on the cross, prefaced by the word 'Father', his favourite form of address to God. As already mentioned, the Church uses the whole verse as a versicle and response in compline. Countless Christians have used it in the past and still do in the present, as a short prayer before falling asleep, and many trusting souls murmur it as they feel the approach of death.

32 Joy after forgiveness

This lovely little psalm is worthy of deep and frequent meditation. Its message is summarized in the opening sentence: 'Blessed is he whose sin is forgiven'. Many commentators relate it to David's sin with Bathsheba (2 Sam. 11), and his later forgiveness (12.13). It develops in succeeding pairs of verses: 1—2 the blessing of forgiveness; 3—4 the psalmist's distress before confession; 5—6 his relief from confession; 7—8 all may experience it; 9—11 God's promise to watch over him and guide him with warning and direction; 12 a bidding to all who are true of heart to share the writer's joy.

There must be absolute sincerity in confession and forsaking sin, each sinner must be one in whom there is no guile, a quality which Jesus recognized and commended in Nathaniel (John 1.47).

While the psalmist was reluctant to confess, he experienced a heaviness of heart which affected his physical well-being. Fortunately, he felt God's hand heavy upon him, a continuous pressure to confess his sin.

When he did so, without attempting to hide anything, he felt immediate relief and experience of God's forgiveness.

So he urges everyone to have the same experience of God and to pray when trouble comes. Then the waves that beat upon us from time to time will not only not overwhelm us but not reach us. We shall feel God's protecting care at every step.

In verses 9—11 the writer hears God speaking within him, promising God's knowledge of his situation and God's instruction and direction. He is warned that he must not be like horses, which need to be curbed with bit and bridle until they go where the driver directs. Both faithful and godless people are told of the consequences of their actions: the former feel embraced by God, the latter find life a succession of trials and troubles.

In the final verse all who are true of heart are promised that they will experience the writer's relief and joy, and like him be loud in the praise of God.

33   National thanksgiving

This psalm is a jubilant song of praise for some unspecified national victory, as is made clear by the use of the first person plural. In the opening three verses all upright men in Israel are called to sing a new song, with the implication that God is not only to be praised for mercies in the past, but for fresh occasions in the present.

The main body of the psalm, verses 4–18, shows why praise is due to God – his work in creation, his rule over the nations, his characteristics of righteousness, justice and loving kindness, his eternal purposes. The Lord surveys all the inhabitants of the earth, he knows all that they do. Nations must not put their trust in armies nor in cavalry. God takes note of how they employ the power with which he has endowed them. His special care is for those whom he has chosen to be his own people, but it is wider than this, and includes all who trust in his unfailing love, to feed them in times of scarcity and to save them when there is a threat of death.

In verses 19–21 choir and people respond to this call to worship in a chorus of praise, hailing God as both shield and helper, declaring that they have waited eagerly for him, trusting in his Name, the revelation of his character and will.

So they conclude with the prayer that God's merciful kindness may always be upon them, for all their hope is in him.

34   Praise at all times

This psalm covers all kinds of experiences, and the writer calls to all who glory in God 'O praise the Lord with me, and let us exalt his name together'. It is an acrostic in the Hebrew, with each verse beginning with a new letter of the alphabet. Possibly because of that fact, it does not fall into easily perceivable sections.

The writer bears witness that whenever he sought help from the Lord, he felt himself freed from fear, a consequence that anyone would feel was truly an answer from God (v.4). Whenever one looks to God, his face is freed from anxiety and becomes bright with joy (v.5). The angel of the Lord encamps in protection around those who revere him (v.6), angels being thought of as God's agents in dealing with men. Readers of the psalm are urged 'O taste and see that the Lord is good', meaning to accept the test of experience (v.8). God not only protects, he provides as well, so that those who trust him lack nothing good (see psalm 23).

The psalmist urges his pupils to listen to him if they want to enjoy life. They should keep from lying, turn away from evil, create harmony. He warns them that God is against all evil doers. On the other hand God comes to the rescue of the righteous, and heals the broken hearted. He promises that the righteous will survive their troubles by God's grace, while the ungodly will succumb to them.

The writer has justified the first verse of his psalm: 'I will bless the Lord continually, his praise shall be always in my mouth'.

35   Prayer under attack

This psalm is said by many to be David's appeal to God for help when he was hunted by Saul. That may be so, but it could equally be the prayer of a good man trying to live a neighbourly and helpful life among unscrupulous and malicious enemies. He appeals to God to be both a large shield to defend his whole body and a buckler, a small round shield, to defend him against arrows or sudden sword thrusts. He prays to God to stand between him and his attackers.

After this appeal for God's defence, he prays against his enemies — let all who seek his life be confounded, let them be disgraced, let them be like the chaff driven away by the wind, let the avenging angel of the Lord pursue them, let them fall to destruction. Then, says the psalmist, he would rejoice, for he would know that the Lord is a sure deliverer of the poor and needy, from all who oppress them (vv.4–10).

Not only is he attacked with physical violence, but he is falsely accused and mocked at every possible opportunity; in spite of his readiness to help them, his solicitude when they are ill, his sympathy when they are in trouble, they habitually return evil for good. So he wonders how long God will see all this without intervening to defend him. He feels surrounded by hungry lions. If God will come to his rescue, then he will proclaim God's salvation publicly (vv.11–19).

He continues to express his sense of injustice and malice, and begs God not to be silent and leave him undefended, culminating in an almost impatient cry 'Bestir yourself, awake to do me right, O Lord my God!'

He knows that he has friends, who long to see him vindicated, who will rejoice when this happens and acknowledge that he takes delight in his faithful servant's welfare. As for himself, he will praise God, who will have been seen to be working for his good all day long. His joyful, grateful heart will overflow with thanksgiving and he will talk to all when he knows of God's righteousness and vindication (vv.20–29).

36 God's goodness and man's sinfulness

This poem begins with a portrait of the godless, but soon turns from man's sinfulness to the goodness of God. The wicked man has no fear of God, he boasts about himself, his words are full of deceit, he plots all kinds of evil, even in his bed, his conscience is so dulled that he does not turn away from evil (vv.1−4).

Among the characteristics of God he mentions his unfailing kindness, his righteousness like a great mountain, his justice as extensive as the ocean, his care for all his creatures and, most precious of all, his tenderness in sheltering those who come to him for protection under his warm wings. Good things and delightful things flow from him as a river. He is like a fountain of life, both physical and spiritual. In his light we are able to perceive the mysteries and purpose of life. So the psalmist prays that God will continue all this kindness and mercy (vv.5−10).

He goes on to pray that the upright in heart may be defended against 'the foot of pride', which tramples on the weak, and that evil men may be defeated and their power over others broken (vv.11−12).

We who study this psalm today can rejoice with him in the revelation of God's goodness and resolve by God's grace to grow like him.

37 Waiting for God

This is a teaching poem rather than a prayer, a vindication of God's ways to man, dealing with the prosperity of the wicked and the trials of the righteous. It is akin in subject matter to psalm 73 and reminiscent of the two ways in psalm 1.

The writer has been deeply troubled by the comparative prosperity of men who did not value religion or practise morality. As he ponders this problem he comes to the conclusion that if one waits patiently, one will see that righteous adjustment will take place in this life and sin will be visited on the wicked and his posterity.

The message of the psalm is in verse 1, 'Do not vie with the wicked: or envy those that do wrong'. One rather regrets the disappearance of 'Fret not thyself' (BCP) meaning 'don't get all worked up and angry, don't be envious about the ill-deserved prosperity and success of evil doers', but 'Trust in the Lord and do good' (v.3) – delight in the Lord (v.4), commit your way unto him (v.5) and you will find satisfaction and happiness (v.6), trust in God and wait patiently for him to act.

In the Hebrew this psalm is an acrostic, each succeeding stanza of varying lines, beginning with a fresh letter of the alphabet. It may be divided into four almost equal sections: verses 1–11 give positive teaching and advice; verses 12–22 describe the fate which will overtake the wicked; verses 23–31 list the rewards which will be given to the righteous; verses 32–40 describe the final result when the wicked shall be destroyed and the righteous find their salvation and stronghold in the Lord.

Verse 13 'The Lord shall laugh him to scorn'. In the light of the New Testament revelation of God in Jesus Christ, we cannot imagine God doing this. Verse 21 says that the wicked borrow but never repay, whereas the righteous give generously and graciously. Verse 23 declares that the feet of the godly are made firm and steady by the Lord who takes delight in him. Even if he falls, it will be little more than a stumble, for the Lord will have his hand on him. Verse 25 makes clear that the writer is an old man, who claims that he has never seen the righteous forsaken or his children begging their bread. The reader today, thinking of the hungry nations, wishes that this was always so. Yet this psalmist clearly believes that God never forsakes those who trust him, as some other psalmists seem to fear. There is no idea in this psalm of an after-life in which the inequalities of which he is conscious may be set right.

Jesus knew this psalm, for he quotes verse 11 as one of the beatitudes in the Sermon on the Mount (Matt. 5.5). His own trust in the Father went much further than this psalm, for he was ready to go to a painful, shameful death to prove God's love and forgiveness, leaving the consequences in the Father's hands.

38 In a serious illness

The speaker is seriously ill and, like the people of his own time, believes that his illness is God's punishment for his sin. In the opening words of his prayer, identical with the opening verse of psalm 6, he prays that God's fierce anger against him and his sin may cease.

In verses 2–8 he describes his sufferings. His flesh is unhealthy with festering sores, his bones ache, his limbs are inflamed, sudden pains shoot through his body as if he were struck by arrows, God's arrows. He is left exhausted and helpless. He believes that the cause of his suffering is his sins which have overwhelmed him like a flood. At the end of this section he says: 'I cry aloud in the yearning of my heart', yearning for relief, and perhaps also for forgiveness.

The consciousness of that takes him back to God and he realizes that God knows his inmost feelings, deep and confused as they are. He gets no help from friends and relatives and there are enemies who whisper against him and even seek his life. His heart faints, his spirit is disquieted, his sight and hearing are affected and he doesn't feel able to confide his distress in others (vv.9–14).

His only resort is God for he can expect no mercy from men. He is near to breaking point. Verse 18 begins to bring relief: 'I acknowledge my wickedness, and I am filled with sorrow at my sin'. Deep in his heart, he knows that he seeks only for good, in contrast to his enemies who repay evil for good. So he can now pray to God, not to forsake him, but to come speedily to his help, for God alone is his hope and salvation.

39 The uncertainty of life

'A saint, sorely exercised by the problems of life, restrains his moanings and complaints in the presence of the ungodly, lest his words should do harm. So Job in his earlier trials "sinned not with his lips, did not charge God with foolishness", but in silence "received evil" at the hands of the Lord' (Job 6.22, 2.10). In these words a Biblical scholar, Dr W. T. Davidson, summed up the message of this moving psalm in a minor key.

In verses 1–3 the sufferer describes how he suffered in silence, but finally his heart grew hot within him and he could keep silent no longer.

In verses 4–7 he tells that he knows that life is short, especially compared with God's eternity, and prays that God will let him know how short his time is, so that he can live accordingly. He knows that it is no good heaping up riches, for he cannot be sure that he will be the one to make use of them.

Verse 8 is the heart of the psalm: 'And now Lord, what is my hope? Truly my hope is in you.' So he prays that he may be delivered from all his sins and not made the butt of fools. He suffers physically, but admits that both his bodily pain and mental anguish are God's punishment for sin. As he surveys his life, he knows how short and fleeting it is, and that he himself is but a transient creature (vv.8−12).

In the last three verses he prays for pardon and a renewal of health, pleading 'For I am but a stranger with you' and therefore with a right to God's protection. He realizes that he is only a temporary dweller upon earth, a passing guest who stays a short time and then is quickly forgotten. As a result of his prayer his spirit brightens up, he begins to smile again, before he leaves this life and is no more. No firm belief in an after life has yet dawned in his mind or the minds of his contemporaries. As one reads this psalm or hears it sung in the worship of the Church, one begins to get the feeling that the writer's hope in God was not less but more than those of us who have the assurance of the New Testament; that God has prepared a future for all who trust him, and also for those who do not yet do so.

40   Joy in God's will

The most noticeable thing about this psalm is the sudden change of mood that comes at verse 14. The first part of it is a thanksgiving for God's help in the past and an expression of joyful readiness to do God's will. The second part, verses 14−19, is an urgent appeal for further help. These later verses are almost identical with psalm 70 and may have been a separate psalm at first. On the other hand the writer's circumstances may have changed drastically, moving him to urgent prayer that God will come to his rescue again. The last three verses show a quiet trust in God once more and are a prayer for

51

all believers, yet the psalmist is still conscious of his own desperate situation and the need of immediate help.

Verses 6–7 speak of the wonders that God has wrought in the past and of the confidence that God's thoughts are still on him. God's marvels are more than he is able to express. There is no one who can be compared with God.

In verses 8–9 he sees that God does not demand animal sacrifices, but an open ear to hear his word and be obedient to his Law. His answer to God is 'Lo I come'. We may remember the young Isaiah, present at the morning sacrifice in the Temple, when the smoke of the sacrifice seemed to merge into the brightness of heaven. As a result, when God appeals for a messenger whom he can send to his sinful people, he, like the psalmist, responds 'Here am I, send me!' (Isa. 6.1–8).

A deeper thought may come as one remembers the response of Mary of Nazareth to the experience which Christians speak of as the Annunciation: 'Behold, I am the handmaid of the Lord; let it be to me according to your word' (Luke 1.38).

Verse 10 is the key verse of this psalm. The writer has often held the scroll of the Law (*Torah*) in his hand and felt a personal message to himself that he should do God's will. His response is 'O my God I long to do it, your law delights my heart'. The writer of the Epistle to the Hebrews quotes these words, as said by Christ, summing up his glad obedience to God's will (Heb. 10.7).

Verses 11–13: The psalmist is not satisfied in benefiting from God's mercies within himself. He wishes to speak of them to others. In these verses he speaks of telling 'the great congregation' of God's faithfulness and loving kindness. He wants to make his gratitude widely known to his fellow-worshippers.

Verse 14: He prays in a new situation of the need that God will continue to protect him.

Verses 15–17: He recognizes that his troubles are largely the consequences of his many sins; his heart fails him as he remembers them.

This is a most valuable insight for believers in every generation, not that God is punishing them for their sins, but that their troubles are a consequence of wrong doings. We have largely brought them on ourselves. So he prays to God to deliver him and come to his immediate help.

Verses 18–19: He is conscious of critics and enemies who seek to harm him, who wish him evil, who taunt him with 'Aha! Aha!' He prays that they may be put to shame when they see God's saving love towards him.

In the last three verses he prays for all fellow-believers in God whose verdict will be 'God is great', a verse which our Muslim friends will appreciate in their conviction that 'God is the greatest'.

The last verse of this psalm combines faith and urgency: 'You are my helper and my deliverer, make no long delay O Lord my God!'

41 In sickness, enmity and betrayal

Rabbi Cohen's summary can hardly be improved upon: 'Another psalm relating to a time of sickness when the patient's suffering was aggravated by mental uneasiness over the machinations of enemies. In particular one man whom he considered a close friend had proved traitorous.'

The first three verses speak of the divine blessings which the merciful receive and enjoy: deliverance when troubles come to them, protection against their enemies. His life when threatened is preserved, a happiness which others will perceive, an indication of divine support.

In verses 4–9 the writer describes the malice of his enemies, who wish him harm and long for his death, who even come to visit him on his sick bed and hypocritically wish him well, but secretly hope for the worst, who, when they go out, whisper malicious thoughts and false accusations. He is most hurt by the conduct of one whom he regarded as a bosom friend, who now turns against him and tries to bring about his disgrace, perhaps by inferring that his illness is due to hidden sin. The psalmist himself admits that there may be some truth in this, for he prays 'O Lord, be merciful toward me, heal me for I have sinned against you' (v.4).

After this expression of grief for the ill-will of enemies and the betrayal by the friend whom he trusted, he returns to his prayer and asks that God will raise him up (from his sick bed) so that he may requite these false 'friends', when he will know that God delights in him and does not allow his enemies to triumph, but upholds him in his integrity and assures him that the divine presence is always with him.

The last verse of the psalm does not seem to follow quite logically. It is said to be a doxology and blessing of God for the first book of the five collections of psalms into which the Psalter is divided, this psalm being the closing one of the first collection.

Jesus almost certainly knew this psalm, for he models one of the beatitudes on its opening verse: 'Blessed are the merciful, for they shall obtain mercy'. Also in one of his graphic parables, that known as 'the unmerciful servant', he drives home the lesson that his disciples must not only be forgiven, but also forgiving. Otherwise, we move outside the circle of God's forgiveness.

54

'No more vivid simile' says Rabbi Cohen, 'could be imagined: a thirsty timid hind fearful of attack at a pool or stream by stronger animals which congregate there yet driven by the instinct of self-preservation to find the water that is essential to life. It offers a most striking analogy to the psalmist, hunted by enemies, who feels he cannot live without the spiritual refreshment which he draws from the Temple.'

He speaks of a desperate thirst for God and longs to find himself again in the presence of God. Night and day he mourns his sad plight, mocked by enemies 'Where is now your God?', implying that God is either powerless to help him or has withdrawn his love. He sadly remembers earlier pilgrimages to the Temple when he joined with many others in festival procession and thanksgiving.

In verses 6 and 7 he addresses his soul rather reproachfully, trying to discover the cause of his depression. This is a searching exercise for any despondent soul, and may reveal reasons for the disquiet. I may feel that I have been over-looked, or that someone has been praised for what I have done or been given the task I would have liked to do. To find a reason is halfway to the cure. On the other hand, I may find no reason for my depression, and then I have to answer as the psalmist did: 'O put your trust in God, for I will praise him yet who is my deliverer and my God'.

In verses 8–12 he reverts again to his heaviness of heart. He seems to be far away in the north near the mountain ranges of the Hermons or on the other side of Jordan. He feels like one almost overwhelmed with storms and buffeted with waves. Yet he knows that God is his Rock, the strength of his life, and he needs God to be with him day and night. He feels that God has forgotten him. Perhaps he did not remember when Jerusalem was desolate and its people cried out 'The Lord has forsaken me; my God has forgotten me', and the prophet heard God's words of comfort 'Behold I have graven you on the palms of my hands' (Isa. 49.16). Entire cities or individual souls are always held in divine remembrance.

In verse 12, he speaks again of his pain and the mocking of his enemies. In the final two verses he again asks his question and answers it with the same words of trust.

Whenever I read this psalm, I ask myself if I long for God with the same deep longing as the poet who wrote it.

43 Similar circumstances?

This psalm might originally have been part of the preceding one, or it might have been written by someone in similar circumstances of trial and depression. He appeals to God to vindicate him and longs to return home. Although he acknowledges God as his refuge, he fears that God has turned away from him. As a result, he goes about sadly like a mourner at a funeral.

Verse 3 is one of the loveliest prayers in the Psalter, in which the psalmist pictures twin angels of God's presence bringing him light and truth and guiding him to the divine dwelling place.

Verse 4: Then, he will come to God's altar with joy and praise him to the sweet accompaniment of his harp, murmuring 'O God, my God!'

Verse 5: For the time being, he cannot shake himself out of his mood of despondency, and asks the same question asked twice already in psalm 42.

Verse 6: He makes the same answer as that twice

made by the previous (or same) writer: 'O my soul, put your trust in God, my rescuer and my God!'

44   A national lament

This psalm is not a personal lament but the cry of a nation in desperate straits after defeat in battle. The nation at the time of writing is defended by 'our armies'. The psalmist's complaint is that God did not go out with those armies (v.10), and the whole nation has been humiliated, in spite of the fact that it has been faithful to the national covenant with God and not worshipped strange gods (vv.17 and 20). Yet defeat has made them a byword among the nations.

The opening verses (1–4) look back on God's help in the past, especially on the entry into the promised land and their settlement there. God's favour enabled them to defeat all enemies and 'to root and grow'.

Verses 5–9 tell how, in their early years as a nation, they did not trust in armed might but in God alone, and they have never ceased to be thankful to him for their early victories.

But now things have changed: it looks as if God has cast them off, allowing them to be butchered, so that they have become a laughing stock to surrounding nations. They feel shamed, forsaken and disgraced (vv.10–17).

The writer feels that this desperate humiliation has not been deserved, for the nation has not forgotten God nor has it strayed from his paths. And yet . . . and yet, the bitterness of defeat and the shadow of death have fallen upon them: 'It is for your sake' that all this has happened, and they seem to be little better than sheep destined for slaughter (vv.18–23).

In the closing four verses the psalmist calls to God to

wake from his apparent sleep, to hide his face from them no longer, forgetful of their plight. 'Rouse yourself O Lord!' is his cry of panic, 'arise and help us', O God of mercy. That very prayer is a sign of both the writer's and the nation's continuing trust.

45 Anthem for a royal wedding

The occasion of this psalm is the wedding of a Hebrew king to a foreign princess. It could have been the marriage of Solomon to a daughter of a Pharaoh of Egypt, or Ahab's marriage to Jezebel (see v.12). In it there is praise for the bridegroom, a welcome to the bride and an exhortation to her to forget her own country and make herself at home in her new one, and finally a prayer for the happiness of both.

In the first verse the writer says his heart is moved by the occasion; his mind has been thinking of fine phrases for his poem and he is confident of being able to say something appropriate.

Verses 2–9 are in praise of the king, somewhat flattering perhaps, as all such occasions tend to be. He is the most handsome of men, a gracious speaker, a fine soldier, a confident leader, well able to defeat his enemies. His throne is given him by God, so his subjects expect him to 'ride on in truth and for the sake of justice'. The sceptre which he holds in his hand is a symbol and a pledge of righteousness. His robes are magnificent, scented with perfumed spices; his palaces are inlaid with ivory (see 1 Kings 22.39). Princesses from neighbouring countries have come to the wedding; and above all, standing by him is the bride in her wedding robe of cloth of gold, the gold coming from Ophir, famed for the finest of all precious metals.

The court poet goes on to welcome the bride, and expresses the expectation that, from now on, she will identify herself with the nation over which her husband reigns. She may have had to leave her father's country and she will now have sons who may become princes in other lands. Her bridal attire is described and her attendant bridesmaids, or ladies in waiting, will escort her to the king's palace. The king, her husband, gazes admiringly at her beauty. He desires her with all his heart.

In the final verse, the poet comes back to the king whose fame, he promises, shall be remembered all down the future generations, praised by his people for ever. The people of Britain remember the shouts at the coronation of every monarch – and most recently – 'God save the Queen. May the Queen live for ever'.

46 God our stronghold

There seems to be almost complete agreement among biblical scholars that this psalm, and the two that follow it, refer to the occasion in Hezekiah's reign when Jerusalem was threatened by the invasion of Sennacherib and wonderfully delivered by divine intervention. The keynote of it is that God is our stronghold, a theme which Luther developed in one of his great hymns, 'A safe stronghold our God is still'.

The first three verses speak of God as a very present help in trouble, ever ready to come to the rescue of his people. Though the earth may be shaken by some convulsion of nature and mountains disappear into the sea, whatever may happen, God's people need have no fear.

Verses 4–7 are a contrast to the stormy ocean as God's presence is described as a peaceful river fertilizing the countryside and bringing refreshment to the people of the city (see Isaiah 8.6, where Shiloah's gently flowing stream is contrasted with Assyria's mighty river. See also 33.21). God is in the midst of the holy city and as long as she remains faithful to him no power can prevail over her. The BCP declares that God will help her 'right early'. The ASB states 'at break of day'. Although there may be unrest among the nations, God thunders and the whole universe trembles before him. The antiphon from the choir is

'The Lord of hosts is with us: the God of Jacob is our stronghold.'

In verses 8–11 the psalmist draws out the lessons of the wonderful thing that has happened. The powerful Assyrian army has been routed, their bows are broken, their spears snapped in two, their chariots of war and their supply waggons burnt with fire. So God will make wars to cease in all the world, a promise that has not yet been fulfilled, though modern weapons and nuclear bombs make us more aware of the threatening horrors of modern war. The psalmist therefore calls to the nations to desist and give up their vain strivings: 'Be still then and know that I am God'. There is a deeper meaning to this urging, for people are learning to be still in the realization of God's presence, and in silence listen to his message for each present time.

Twice in this short psalm we get a mention of God as the Lord of hosts, a title which is used nearly 300 times in the Old Testament. Originally it had a military significance, the God of armies, especially the armies of Israel. Gradually it came to mean something more spiritual – Lord of the armies of holy ones, prophets and saints, always on God's side in the struggle between good and evil. In the story of Elisha in Dothan, besieged by the army of Syria, the prophet prays that the Lord will open his young attendant's eyes. When he does so, all the hills around are seen crowded with heavenly chariots (2 Kings 6.15–17). Both this psalm and the Elisha incident assert the omnipotence and sovereignty of the great ruler of all, whose will is that wars shall cease and his rule be accepted. The psalm ends with the repetition of its earlier refrain:

'The Lord of hosts is with us: the God of Jacob is our stronghold.'

47   God king of the nations

This psalm is recited in the synagogue before the blowing of the *Shofar* (ram's horn) on New Year's day in the Jewish calendar. It is also appointed by the Christian Church for recital on Ascension Day. Its theme is God's universal supremacy. It celebrates the defeat of Assyria mentioned in psalm 46, and is a call to all nations to acknowledge his divine sovereignty over the whole earth. It may be divided into three sections.

Verses 1–5: A call to the nations to shout for joy as when a king ascends his throne, perhaps recalling the crowning of Israel's first king when the greeting shouted was 'Long live the King!' (1 Sam. 10.24). The Lord Most High is pictured as ascending his throne after his victory over the nations and his choice of Israel as his favoured nation.

Verses 6–7: Praises to God the King of all the earth in a well-chosen psalm, beautifully rendered by choir and orchestra.

Verses 8–10: God is enthroned over the nations, and their leaders come together with Israel, the people of the God of Abraham, through whom all are to receive a blessing (Gen. 18.18).

Two comments might be made about this psalm. The

61

first is that it is prophetic, looking forward to a time of victory as if it was already happening.

The second is that it depicts things happening in the celestial sphere, much as they happen in the terrestrial. God comes down from his throne to intervene on behalf of his people and having done so, he goes up again to his holy and eternal throne.

The last verse of the psalm expresses its message and meaning:

'For the mighty ones of the earth are become the servants of God, and He is greatly exalted.'

48   God protects Zion

This is the third of the trio of psalms celebrating the defeat of Sennacherib and the Assyrians. Jerusalem is the city of the great king, it is under God's protection, and there is the joyful hope that it will always be so.

Verses 1–3 speak of God dwelling in Zion. The ASB describes it as 'where godhead truly dwells'. Throughout the city, God is famed for its protection.

Verses 4–8 describe the defeat of the besieging army, struck dumb in astonishment, fleeing in terror, trembling like a woman in childbirth, shattered like ships in a storm. Phrase after phrase is piled up to describe the amazing victory. Now people see God's rescuing power, which they had only heard of before.

Verses 9–13 give thanks in the Temple for this great victory. The hills round Jerusalem are pictured as rejoicing and the villages and little towns of Judah share in the joy.

The worshippers are invited to go round the walls, the protecting towers and ramparts, and the unharmed houses. This victory is something that must be told of to later generations, with the assurance that what has happened on this great occasion will happen repeatedly in the future.

'Great is the Lord, and highly to be praised.'

49   The certainty of mortality

This psalm, like the preceding three, is addressed to all peoples. It calls to all to pay attention, for the writer is going to deal with a mystery, a riddle, a dark saying, a question of universal interest to rich and poor alike. As one reads this psalm, one gets the impression that it is meant more as a warning to people of higher education and especially to the well-to-do.

Verses 1–4 are a call to all peoples to understand, and the psalmist hopes that his meditation will bring understanding.

Verses 5–14 assert that men of great wealth, who for most of their lives have put their trust in riches, cannot live for ever. They, like all others, have to die. All the different versions of the psalm make the same point.

The BCP says 'No man may deliver his brother, nor make agreement unto God for him. For it costs more to redeem their souls, so that he must let that alone for ever' (i.e. redemption is so costly that he must give up the very idea).

'Money cannot purchase the boon of life.' Under the Mosaic law, a man whose ox had gored a neighbour was liable to lose his life, but he might save himself by paying a fine or a ransom, Exod. 21.38–42. But a murderer might not thus purchase immunity from punishment, Num. 35.31. In this case, no brother nor friend, however dear, can be saved from death by the wealthy man, still less can he save himself' (Professor Davidson, *The Psalms*, The Century Bible).

The New English Bible states: 'Alas! no man can ever ransom himself nor pay God the price of that release; his ransom would cost too much, for ever beyond his price to pay, the ransom that would let him live on always and never see the pit of death.'

The Jerusalem Bible has a similar message: 'But no man can redeem himself or pay his own ransom to God, the price for himself is too high; it can never be that he will live on for ever and avoid the sight of the abyss.'

The ASB, on which this series of meditations is based, is equally clear: 'No man may ransom his brother, or give God a price for him, so that he may live for ever; and never see the grave; for to ransom men's lives is so costly: that he must abandon it for ever.'

Wise men must die, as well as the ignorant and foolish, even though estates (and streets!) may be named after them; and a rich man without understanding is no better than beasts that perish.

All are fated to die, going down into the grave (Sheol) like flocks of sheep, their form will disintegrate, all former glory will be lost.

Verses 16–21 hint that there is a more hopeful future for the upright. God will ransom my life. He will receive me when I die. The psalmist, however, is haunted by the fates of the rich, whose wealth and property increase. He can take nothing away with him when he dies, even though he counts himself happy in life and receives the congratulations of others as successful men always do. He will join the company of his fathers, but will never see light, the darkness of the nether-world will be everlasting. Rabbi Cohen in his commentary concludes: 'There is nothing sinful in being rich, and a wealthy man may be as righteous or better than a poor man. When, however, he glories only in material prosperity and fails to appreciate the value of the spiritual and of the moral virtues, he then lacks the understanding of life with its God-given purpose and sublime opportunities. His existence is merely animal and he perishes like the beast.'

Yet, in all this warning there is a whisper of immortality, the hope that God will ransom each, and rescue each, from the power of the grave. In this a hope is expressed implicitly, which will develop in the later chapters of the Old Testament, and be the Gospel of the New.

50 God's case against Israel

It is now generally agreed that the conditions denounced in this psalm are similar to those which called forth stern teaching from Isaiah, Amos and Hosea. So it would seem reasonable to date it in the second half of the 8th century BC. The picture aroused in the imagination is of a court where God is both the plaintiff and the judge. God, the Lord, the Mighty One (v.1) summons the earth to stand trial at a great assize.

The four stages of the psalm are:

Verses 1–6: God himself is the judge.
        7–15: God speaks.
     16–22: He accuses Israel of disobedience and hypocrisy.
     23–24: A warning not to forget God, but to honour him by keeping to his paths.

Verse 2: God calls out of Zion, from which the Shechinah (glory) and Torah (law) go forth to the world.

Verse 4: The message is not only to Israel, but to all mankind.

Verse 3: Peals of thunder and flashes of lightning are symbols of his presence.

Verse 5: Those who have made a covenant with him are called to account.

Verse 6: The accused are assured of a fair judgment, for God is righteous.

Verse 8: The sacrifices have been offered regularly, God does not reproach them for failure to do this.

Verses 9—13: God the Creator needs no food from men.

Verse 14: The sacrifice that God desires is a heart grateful for all his love and faithfulness to the vows made to him.

Verse 15: Then they may call upon him in times of trouble and he will come to their rescue.

Verses 16—22: The sins which are specified are those committed against their neighbour, or their apparent acquiesence in the deeds of evil men.

Verse 21: In this they were guilty of thinking of God as no better than themselves.

Verse 22: God now sets their deeds clearly before them and finds them guilty.

Verses 23—24: Those who honour God and walk in his ways will be shown his salvation.

51 The cry of a penitent

The Hebrew Psalter has two introductory verses for this psalm: 'A Psalm of David; when Nathan the prophet came to him, after he had gone in to Beer-Sheba'. It might well have added 'and had conspired the murder of Uriah'. Some modern commentators believe that it is much later in date. But the thoughtful readers and perennial penitents will see a spiritual connection between the psalm and the biblical account in 2 Sam. 12.1—13. Later writers may well have seen new personal relevance and deeper meaning as they made this prayer their own.

A deep consciousness of sin and of the need for cleansing and forgiveness permeates the whole soul. In every generation since, countless souls have found that its wording expresses their own sense of guilt and their longing for forgiveness. The penitent today realizes with the writer that ritual sacrifices are not enough, and the sacrifice most acceptable to God is a heart reduced to tears of spirit, as well as of eyes, by the realization of the awfulness of actual sins and a deep longing for forgiveness. The psalm falls into three parts:

Verses 1–12: Prayer for pardon.
             13–17: Resolve for the future.
             18–19: Adaptation for corporate and national penitence.

Verse 4 asserts that all sin is ultimately sin against God, and confession is the acknowledgment of God's holiness, a recognition that God is right in his judgment on sin.

Verse 5 is an admission that human beings are prone to sin, that fallenness is common to all, rather than the claim that the marital act is sinful.

Verse 6 describes God's requirement that man must be ruthlessly truthful about himself, absolutely sincere in himself before God and in relation to others. When this is offered to God, he grants spiritual wisdom and guidance in all problems and perplexities.

Verse 7: Hyssop was prescribed for cleansing after contact with a leper or a corpse, and the psalmist prays to be purified figuratively in the same way. The Christian will remember Jesus touching the leper and taking the hand of the little daughter who had just died and touching the bier of the body of the widow's son at Nain, on the way to the graveyard. 'Whiter than snow' will remind the penitent of the promise in Isa. 1.18.

Verses 10–12 are the heart of this psalm and should be memorized for frequent praying.

Verse 12: The BCP states, 'stablish me with thy free spirit'. Rabbi Cohen has 'let a willing spirit uphold me', Moffat 'give me a willing spirit as my strength', all three, as well as the ASB, implying 'ready obedience'.

Verse 14: 'Blood guiltiness' in the BCP is replaced by 'bloodshed' in the ASB. It may have the deeper meaning of 'mortal sin', for ultimately persistent sin of any kind damages and kills the life of the soul. St John in his first Epistle speaks of a 'sin unto death' (5.16), and the writer of the Epistle to the Hebrews emphasizes the danger of repeated sin, and says that in sin we crucify the Son of God afresh and 'hold him up to contempt' (6.4–6).

Verses 15–19 speak of the effects of God's forgiveness – a grateful, praising heart, a humble readiness to share with others the assurance and experience of God's forgiveness, which can lead them also to turn to God, in penitence for the past, in the happiness of forgiveness, and in an eager, willing spirit for the future.

Jesus taught us that there is only one condition for forgiveness, and that is willingness to forgive others the wrongs they do to us. If we are unforgiving, it shows that we do not really understand the meaning of forgiveness; we move outside the circle of forgiveness. If we find it difficult to forgive, we may be helped to do so by remembering the first word from the cross: 'Father, forgive them, for they know not what they do', not only praying for all who in any way had a hand or voice in bringing him there, but also finding excuse for them.

The reader today can be grateful to the original writer of this moving psalm, whoever he was, and heartfeltly grateful to the God of mercy, forgiveness and healing, and to his beloved Son who so wonderfully revealed him in terms of a human life lived out in the same world.

52   An oppresser denounced

The evil doer denounced in this psalm is a man in a
position of power – he is rich and unscrupulous, he
boasts of his ruthless intentions and behaviour, he
works not so much by inflicting physical injury as
through slanderous accusations, he deliberately rejects
what is good and prefers evil. The heading to psalm
identifies him with Doeg the Edomite who gave infor-
mation to Saul about the movements of David (1 Sam.
21.7, 22.9–19) but some commentators think the psalm
is of a much later date.

Its writer is evidently one of the oppressor's victims, a
much humbler person who speaks on behalf of the
righteous sufferers. In verses 1–4 he denounces the 'man
of power' and his cruel, lying ways. In the next three
verses he warns him of his certain fate when God will
destroy him, render him homeless and force him into
banishment, much to the relief and satisfaction of the
godly. In verses 8 and 9, the writer speaks of his own
trust in God, feeling himself as firmly planted and
fruitful as a flourishing olive tree. So he thanks God for
the tyrant's overthrow, urges the faithful to praise God
for what he is doing and will continue to do, and
declares that he will attend God's house and look forward to further demonstrations of God's power.

53   A sad reflection repeated

This psalm is almost a word-for-word repetition of
psalm 14, with very slight changes to make it suit the
new circumstances. To the writer the whole world seems
corrupt and he longs that a message may go out to the
world from Jerusalem.

54   In great danger

This psalm is the prayer of a man in danger from godless enemies who seek to kill him. The title at its heading associates it with Saul's pursuit of David. So many psalms are said to be connected with Saul's persecution that one wonders if David had enough time to plan his escapes. However, his grief at this treatment, and his memories of it, might have inspired brief psalms which expressed his trust in God, thankfulness for God's protection, and the remembrance of prayers prayed on the many occasions.

Verses 1–3 are an urgent prayer on the part of the psalmist for vindication and rescue from violent men, who pay no attention to God and are out to kill him. The remaining three verses speak of his trust that God will help and support him. He prays that God will destroy these ruthless men and that the evil they plot against him will recoil on their own heads. Then, he promises an offering of glad gratitude and a deepening conviction of God's goodness.

The Christian reciting such psalms as this or meditating on them is often troubled at prayers that God will destroy the evil doers. Obviously we should pray that evil may be destroyed and that there may be a change of heart in those who commit it. Those of us who feel uneasy about these prayers for liquidation of enemies and evil doers, may take some comfort in the fact that other psalmists are not as vindictive. The writer of psalm 94, for example, begins his poem with the words 'O Lord God to whom vengeance belongs, 'O God shine out in glory'. We can safely leave things in the hands of the God and Father of Jesus Christ, who wills that all men shall be saved and come to the knowledge of the truth. Blessed is he!

55   Grief over betrayal

This psalm is the prayer of a servant of God, attacked by enemies and deserted by friends, who has been betrayed by a friend whom he trusted. He fears that God may have hidden his face from him and will not hear his prayer. Some scholars have thought that it was a prayer of David when betrayed by Ahitophel in Absalom's rebellion. But the treacherous friend was the writer's equal, a trusted companion who often joined with him in Temple worship. The conditions from which he longs to escape are those in the city, rather than the dangers in flight.

Verses 1–6: The psalmist describes the dangers he is in, the fear and trembling that have come upon him and the real threat of death. In the overwhelming horror he nevertheless cries out to God.

Verses 7–12: He longs for quiet and security and wishes that he could fly away like a wild dove that takes refuge in a cleft of rock, far away from the threats of men and the violent turmoil in the city. His longing for safety and rest has been beautifully expressed in Mendelssohn's anthem 'Oh for the wings, the wings of a dove', the longing even more moving when the words are sung by the pure treble voices of generations of soloist choirboys.

In verses 13–17 the writer's thoughts return to the treachery of the one whom he had trusted as a friend, and in his bitterness he prays that all who live in such an atmosphere of evil may go down in confusion and destruction into death.

His thoughts turn again to God in trust that he will come to his help in spite of his groaning pain at all hours of the day, for which he makes his appeal. As for those who are against him, he can only pray that God will bring them down, for they have no fear of him, and persist in their deceit and violence (vv.13–22).

Another rapid transition follows, and the psalmist addresses himself – 'Cast your burden on the Lord and He will sustain you' – he will not allow the righteous man to stumble and fall (verse 27), a thought taken up in 1 Peter 4.7 'Cast all your anxieties on Him, for He cares for you'.

Yet the psalmist still thinks of divine retribution for the wicked and warns of coming judgment – 'they shall not live out half their days'; he repeats his earlier conviction that God will bring them down to the depths of the pit of death.

For himself, he ends on a note which has been trying to sound throughout the psalm:

'But I will trust in you.'

56   No longer afraid

The writer of this psalm is also a man in great danger, with enemies pressing upon him. He has his times of fear, yet in them all he prays 'I will put my trust in you', knowing that if he does so, he need not fear what men can do to him. He has evidently prayed at the outset of danger and is assured of victory. His psalm is one of praise.

In verses 5–10, he describes the taunting words and plots of his enemies and prays, like the writer of psalm 55, that God will thwart their plans and 'bring them down'. He believes that God has noted his struggle, and that the tears which he has shed in his sufferings will not be forgotten by him. His name will be recorded in God's book of remembrance (cf. Mal. 3.16). So again he resolves to trust in God and not be afraid what mere mortal men can do to him.

The last two verses of the psalm are prayed and written from the standpoint of deliverance already accomplished or in the process of being so. He is ready to fulfil the vows made in his time of desperate need and to offer the appropriate thank-offering prescribed in the ritual of the Temple, as well as loyal obedience to God in the future. He is confident that he is being saved from death, so that he may 'walk before God in the light of the living', meaning the life which is illuminated by the awareness of the divine presence.

There is a suggestion in verse 7 that this psalm may refer to the national sufferings, for the psalmist prays that God will bring down the peoples (plural) in his avenging anger, for there were periods in Israel's history when the nation was in danger from enemies from outside. If this is so, the psalm, though described in the Hebrew heading as a psalm of David, is of a later date.

57 Triumphant trust

The Jewish translation of this psalm attributes it to David when he hid from Saul in the cave near En-gedi (1 Sam. 24.1–7), though the psalmist makes no clear reference to that incident when Saul, unknowingly, was in greater danger from David.

Whoever the writer was, he was still in great danger, comparable to being among ravening lions and enemies armed with sharp swords, spears and arrows (v.5). In his troubles he takes refuge in God, feeling safe under God's overshadowing wings, and confident that God will save him and fulfil his loving purpose for him. The psalm falls into two parts (vv.1–6 and vv.7–12), each of which ends with a magnificent verse of faith and worship. This little creed and gloria is hailed by one commentator 'Greater words than these never came from human lips'.

In the second part, the psalmist is still conscious of danger, but his heart is uplifted to God and fixed there as he reaches for his little harp and greets each morning in thankful praise. He resolves to express his thankful praise publicly. He hopes to do so to nations outside Israel.

The closing five verses of this psalm are repeated as the opening verses of psalm 108, and have been repeated by faithful hearts all down the years since their first utterance. The praising heart today can find no more worshipful words for its early morning meditation.

58   Judges judged

The writer of this psalm is indignant and grieved by the wide corruption that he sees around him. Even judges, whom the Old Testament demands should be incorruptible, are involved. His message to the nation and its judges is that God is the Judge of all the earth, to whom all are answerable.

In verses 1–5, corrupt judges are accused. They are really the rulers of the nation who not only accept bribes to make unjust decisions, but involve themselves in violence. The writer feels they must have been evil from birth. They are as venomous as poisonous snakes and cannot, like most snakes, be controlled by the music of the charmer, because they are deaf to the promptings of conscience.

In verses 6–9, the psalmist uses more metaphors to emphasize their destructive wickedness and the divine retribution. They are as ferocious as young lions whose jaws must be shattered and they must be trodden down and withered like grass. Under God's action they become like a miscarriage, which he thinks of as quickly forgotten. They are swept aside like brambles which are angrily brushed aside from his path by an angry man. He pictures the righteous as rejoicing in such retribution, though he does not pray for all this to happen, but only expects it to do so. His hyperbole is perhaps a measure of his condemnation. The editors of the ASB advise that this psalm be omitted in public worship or personal meditation.

The last verse of the psalm gives its positive message: there is indeed a God who judges the earth and its judges and rulers, and who wills to reward the righteous.

Any idea of forgiveness has not yet appeared in people's thinking. It has certainly not entered into the mind of the writer of psalm 58.

59   More danger

This psalm is a companion to psalm 58. Its writer is pursued by powerful enemies. Its heading is ascribed to David 'when Saul sent, and they watched the house to kill him' (see 1 Sam. 19.11). Verses 6, 12 and 15 suggest that this is not so, though these verses may relate to a later king in danger of defeat and trouble.

In verses 1–6 the psalmist invokes God's help against his enemies. He prays that God will lift him to safety, above the reach of savage men who lie in wait to kill him. They are said to have no justifiable reason for this: he has committed no sin, nor any evil. He prays further that God will come to meet him in his mercy and support.

The title 'Lord of hosts' in the psalms may mean lord

of armies as in 1 Sam. 17.45; it may be used of the
heavenly bodies as in Gen. 2.1; or it could be a reference
to 2 Kings 6.15–17 where Elisha is seen by his young
attendant to be surrounded by chariots of fire. So the
phrase indicates 'the Supreme Ruler of the Universe', a
conclusion borne out by the mention of a desire to
punish all the nations in verse 6.

The enemies in question are likened to a pack of
howling dogs in the gathering gloom, ravenously seeking for food (v.7). They are also described as pouring
out malicious words, believing that God will pay no
heed to the cries of the men they are pursuing.

Verses 9–11 on the other hand, speak of the writer's
confidence that God will intervene and show him the
downfall of his enemies. In verses 12–14 we have his
prayer against the wicked. Death is too good for them,
for people will forget that too easily. They deserve a long
drawn-out punishment. Then men will know that there
is a God who rules and protects Israel.

He returns again to the thought of his enemies as wild
howling dogs roaming the city in search of food. But
quickly he expresses his trust that God will rescue him.
Then, he says, he will sing each day of God's power,
who has been a strong tower and a sure refuge in his
extreme danger (vv.16–20).

The believer, trained and nourished by the God
revealed in the New Testament, must feel resistant to the
idea that God laughs anyone to scorn. He must often
laugh in joy over his creation and in the humorous
situations which he sees in the life of his children. He
must always be grieved about the sinfulness he sees in
the world and always resistant to evil. So even to think
of him laughing anyone to scorn is to be mistakenly and
perversely anthropomorphic. Our thoughts are not his
thoughts!

60 Prayer for restoration

This psalm refers to a time of defeat and humiliation, when the nation is shaken in its confidence, comparable to the effects of an earthquake when rifts open up in the land and buildings crash to the ground. The whole nation staggers like a drunken man and feels that God has deserted it. So the psalmist prays that God will come to their rescue, and prove that they are a people whom he loves (vv.1–5).

The heading to the psalm connects it with David's struggle against Syria at a time when Joab, his general, is facing an attack by Edom.

The writer looks to the past and God's choice of Israel to witness his truth, presenting them, as it were, with a banner which they are to hold before them. He speaks again of Israel as God's beloved people and prays that God will answer his prayer for deliverance (vv.6–7).

He then speaks of God's sovereignty over the tribes of Israel and the surrounding nations, parcelling out their territories. Moab has planned to destroy Israel but it will be like a basin in which the victor washes his feet in menial service. Edom is like a slave to whom the conqueror throws his shoe to clean. The Philistines will tremble at the shouts of triumph (vv.6–10).

Verses 11–14 make clear the difficulties that have to be faced, and assert that God's help is essential for recovery and ultimate victory. Verse 11 speaks of a fortified city in the heart of Edom. This may be a reference to Petra, which pilgrims today still find difficult of access.

With God, however, they will be enabled to fight valiantly: with him victory is not only possible but certain. (It should be noted that verses 8–14 are repeated in psalm 108.7–12.)

In this psalm, the believer in God today will find

confidence and encouragement in the ups-and-downs of life, in misfortunes, in fears about the future and in restoration after past failures. As Paul says in Romans 8, in all that happens we can be more than conquerers, 'nothing can separate us from the love of God in Christ Jesus our Lord'.

61   A royal exile?

This psalm is the prayer of one away from Jerusalem, which he regards as the centre of the earth and a place where there are reminders of God's presence with his people. Verse 2 speaks of him calling to God 'from the ends of the earth', although this may not imply a great distance away, but a measure of the intensity of his longing. It is thought by many to be a prayer of David in the time of Absalom's rebellion, when it would not have been safe to stay in the city.

In verses 1–5, he prays that God will set him on 'a rock higher than I', one that he is not able to reach without divine help. His desire to dwell in God's tent indicates that he knows he will find protection and welcome there. In a further metaphor he trusts that he will find shelter under the hiding of the divine wings (see also 57.2). He adds that in the past God has heard his vows and granted his desire.

In verses 6 and 7, the writer speaks of himself in the third person, thinking of his office of king rather than of his personal needs, assured of a long life, guarded by God's truth and mercy, as promised by God through the prophet Nathan (see 2 Sam. 7.16).

In the last verse he returns to direct speech again, promising to keep the vows made in time of trouble and indeed daily, with the resolve to give praise and thanks to God always.

62   The only refuge

The recurring theme of this psalm is seen in its first verse: 'My soul waits in silence for God, for from Him comes my salvation'. Silence, stillness, waiting trustingly and patiently on God, comprise the writer's advice to himself and others. As a result he knows that God alone is his firm rock, his strong tower, his salvation. So he is never disturbed or hopeless in adverse circumstances. He speaks confidently to those who plot against him, who think that he is like a fence or wall about to collapse with the slightest push. They aim to pull him down 'from his height' which may be his exalted position as king. They indulge in falsehood; outwardly they may speak words of blessing, but in their hearts they curse him (vv.1–4).

In verses 5–8, he repeats his trust in God, as his firm rock, strong tower and protecting shelter, and urges his people to a similar trust in God to whom they can pour out their hearts with all their tensions and fears of what may happen.

In verses 9 and 10, his thoughts return to the godless men: they are nothing more than breath blown away by the wind, placed on the scales they register no weight. They practise dishonesty, even robbery. The readers of the psalm are exhorted not to be envious of their prosperity, nor to make wealth the main object of their lives.

He concludes by emphasizing that what he is proclaiming comes to him from God, who will always decide the future. God's goodness, he says, is constant, and in the end he will judge every man by his deeds. Everyone is answerable to God.

63 Longing for God

This psalm, like 61 and 62, is linked with the period when David was forced to leave Jerusalem. It expresses a deep longing for God and his sanctuary, when the writer is in circumstances of difficulty and danger. All through it, there is a note of devotion which makes it one of the most spiritual songs in the whole Psalter.

Verses 1–5 express his deep longing for the intimate communion with God which he had experienced in the sanctuary. Now hard-pressed in the wilderness, he often feels a deep physical thirst, and weariness of spirit as well. In spite of this, he still blesses God in frequent remembrance and prayer.

Verses 6–9 tell how he remembers God's help in the past when God had been his helper and he had felt safe and warm, sheltered under the divine wings. He meditates in the dark hours of the night and feels nourished and sustained in spirit, as his body does after a satisfying meal.

He goes on to think of the fate of his persecutors whose dead bodies shall be devoured by foxes and jackals. In the final verse he alludes to himself as king as in 61.7, trusting that his life will be preserved for many years ahead, while the deceiving godless men will be silenced.

There are times when believers in God feel dry and cold, when prayer is an effort, and one is tempted to think that prayer at such times is of no value. Psalm 63 comes to our aid with the thought that the very dryness is a thirst for God. At such times, we may not feel much warming of the heart or experience any sense of his presence. All we can offer is our will, but God knows that if he has our will, he can do something with us, to further his own purpose of love for each child and for all his other children.

64   God does judge

The writer of this psalm has suffered at the hands of lawless and unscrupulous men. He describes their wicked plottings, their violent actions, their poisonous words. They have no fear of God or man. He prays that God will hear his prayer, preserve his life, and hide him when the evil doers seek him out to harm and destroy him. As we study the psalm, it looks as if the psalmist's complaint is not only against individuals, but also against a conspiracy or gang of determined and ruthless men who hatch mischievous plots, carefully covered up. There seems to be no limit to their wicked hearts, bearing out the prophet Jeremiah's dictum 'the heart is deceitful above all things, and desperately corrupt; who can understand it?' (17.9).

In the second part of the psalm (vv.7–10), the writer expresses his conviction that God will act, in the end righteousness shall triumph. The Lord will bring the evil-doers down, to the great satisfaction of the righteous.

The outcome will be that all who witness the wicked deeds will be struck with awe and understand more deeply God's work, 'and all the upright of heart shall exult', grateful for the security that comes from God, and glorying in the triumph of right over wrong.

Meditating on this psalm, the believer will be struck with the emphasis on the heart, and the contrast between the inner machinations of the wicked and the upright in heart, and will pray for the clean heart desired by the writer of psalm 51 and the guileless heart which Jesus perceived and praised in one of his earliest disciples Nathaniel bar-Tholomew.

65   A harvest hymn

This psalm falls into three easily observed sections: verses 1−3 praise God in the Temple, as a God who answers prayer, forgives sin and who is open to all mankind, revealing his presence to those who come to worship him; verses 4−7 speak of God's wonderful deeds in the creation of the universe, in the thought of nations far away across the seas, in the wonder of sunrise and the quiet peace of evening; verses 8−13 are a thanksgiving for harvest, which is brought about by the rain, which people, at the time of the writer, thought came from the river of God, softening the soil and fertilizing growth, crowning every year with goodness and plenty.

Evidently the year in question was one of a bountiful harvest where there was plenty of good pasture in the untended wilderness, with corn ripening in the valleys, the hillsides planted with vines and trees, and meadows dotted with sheep and lambs. The psalmist's heart is so filled with thanksgiving and joy as he surveys it all, that he pictures hillsides and valleys shouting with joy and harvest hymns.

At seed time and harvest the worshipper is conscious of his dependence on God, the soil, the rain, the sunshine and his own labours, all co-operating in the provision of food for all God's children. As Jesus taught, there is such a bountiful return − thirty, sixty and even one hundred fold. In addition there is all the beauty and

variety of flowers, speaking of a God of beauty, as well
as generosity. Further still, there is the harvest of goodness in the character and heart of man, suggesting that
God has implanted a seed of divinity in every human
being: 'My God, how wonderful Thou art!'

66 Praise for deliverance

The theme of this psalm is thanksgiving for a safe ending
to some national crisis. The first eleven verses strike a
note of national thanksgiving, the last eight verses have
a personal note about them.

There are two verses in this psalm which have a
parallel in the account in Isaiah 37 and 38 of the
deliverance from Sennacherib's invasion: namely, verse
3 is similar to Isaiah 37.20, and verse 17 echoes Isa.
38.3. This suggests that Hezekiah may be the king who
gives personal thanks to God in the second half.

The national thanksgiving in the first half falls into
three sections, verses 1—3 being a call to all the earth to
praise God; verses 4—6 which tell of God's mighty acts,
instancing the journey through the Red Sea and the
crossing of the Jordan into the promised land, and
concluding with the insight that God watches over all
the nations. Verses 7—11 are a thanksgiving for God's
deliverance, who has proved his people as silver is tried;
verse 11, which states 'You let men ride over our heads',
gives a picture of wounded men lying helpless while
horsemen ride pitilessly over them.

In the second half, the individual thanksgiving
(vv.12—14) speaks of the king fulfilling the vows made
during the struggle, and his grateful tribute to God's aid,
voicing his gratitude that God has heard his prayer and
shown his steadfast love.

So the individual today in some disaster or act of

terrorism involving many people, will want to give thanks for his safe escape, and thank God also for the heroic efforts of those coming to the rescue.

67   Universal praise and blessing

This psalm is a prayer for salvation in the widest sense, not only for Israel, but for all nations. In the Jewish liturgy it is recited at the end of the sabbath, as a thanksgiving for the day of rest and worship, but looking forward to the working days of the week which follow. It combines faith in God, thanksgiving for his graciousness, and assurance of his continued blessing.

Verses 1 and 2 are a recognition of God. The writer has the priestly blessing of Num. 6.24–25 in mind: 'The Lord bless you and keep you: the Lord make his face to shine upon you, and be gracious to you: the Lord lift up his countenance upon you and give you peace'.

The ASB speaks of God's liberating power, of which Christians in South America and elsewhere are so conscious – liberation from oppression, hunger, disease and anxiety, a blessing that follows the knowledge of God and his ways.

Verses 3–5: All nations are called to thanksgiving and praise and to accept his righteous government of the world. Verse 3 is repeated in verse 5, emphasizing the key message of this psalm.

Verse 6 declares that the fruitfulness of the earth will follow living in God's way, a fulfilment of the promise in psalm 85.11. Truth will spring from the earth and God in his righteousness will look down in satisfaction and approval. So the worshippers lift grateful trusting hearts to 'God our God'.

Verse 7 is not so much a prayer, but a declaration of

faith and hope, in the assurance that it is God's will to bless the whole earth and all its peoples.

This psalm is widely chosen for singing on harvest festivals, but it is more than a thanksgiving on such occasions, it is recognition of God's love for all peoples, throughout all generations.

68   God's triumphant march

'Whensoever composed, inspired by whatsoever reminiscences of past history or expectations of returning prosperity, this Psalm stands as a monument of the invincible faith and inextinguishable hopes of Israel, and a prophecy of spiritual glories in part realised, in part yet to come!' This tribute of a Christian scholar (Professor Davison in the Century Bible) is quoted by Jewish writers with approval. Rabbi A. Cohen in his commentary after quoting it, adds his own key for interpretation to Jews and Christians alike: 'The basic theme is the triumphant march of God through the past history of Israel as the Hope of his Kingship over all the earth in the future'.

It is headed 'A Psalm of David, a Song', without offering any clue to the actual occasion on which it was composed. It may have been to celebrate one of David's victories over the Philistines, or equally appropriate for the great day when the Ark was brought to Jerusalem.

It divides up into sections which cover the thousand years up to the time of David. These are:

Verses 1–6: God's coming in majesty and power.
        7–18: A review of past history.
        19–23: God also delivers in the present and in the future.
        24–27: The procession of the tribes into the Temple.

85

28–31: A call to all nations to join, bringing their offerings.

32–35: All nations will acknowledge the awe-inspiring nature of the God of Israel.

The first verse of the psalm is an exact repetition of the words of Moses, used whenever the Ark set out on a further stage of its journey. See Num. 10.35.

Verses 5–6 are a lovely description of God's care for his people, from his holy heaven. cf. Isa. 57.15.

Verse 7: In retrospect, the journey through the wilderness, painful and slow as it must have sometimes seemed, is described as a triumphant march of God.

Verse 11 speaks of the thrill of the advancing Israelites as the news spread through the host that Kings and their armies were fleeing before them.

Verse 13 echoes psalm 74.19, which speaks of Israel as God's turtle dove, and pictures flights of doves, covered with silver plumage, with wings of gold.

Verse 15 probably refers to Mount Hermon towering over the surrounding country of Bashan.

Verse 17 reminds us that the protecting chariots of God are as many as 20,000. (See Elisha's vision in 2 Kings 6.16–17.)

Verses 19 and 20 speak splendidly of God as the burden-bearer and the rescuer from death, whereas 21 and 23 reflect a desire for cruel revenge on the oppressors, humanly understandable, but not to be attributed to God.

Verses 24–27 give a vivid picture of the procession of tribes to the Temple, led by a choir of singers, followed by a band of musicians and accompanied by women clashing their timbrels, as Miriam and her attendants are said to have done after the safe crossing of the Red Sea. (See Exod. 15.20–26.) The mentions of the Temple in this psalm suggest that its final version must have been rather later than David.

86

The final verses envisage the kings of the earth coming to Jerusalem with their presents, representing their submission to God's rule.

Verse 30 calls to God to 'rebuke the beast of the reeds'. This probably refers to the hippopotamus, as the symbol of Egypt. The rulers of the nations are likened to wild bulls, and are condemned for their greed for booty and their readiness for war.

Throughout this great psalm of national praise, God is pictured as giving protection, strength and victory to Israel, but inflicting terror and defeat on Israel's enemies.

69 Under cruel treatment

Rabbi Cohen, one of the great Jewish commentators of the psalms, has this moving summary of its contents: 'A deeply pathetic human document is presented by this Psalm. A devout servant of God is undergoing cruel treatment and feels that his sufferings are due to his religious loyalty. He pleads with God for relief and, in burning indignation, begs that retribution come upon his persecutors. His faith remains firm through the ordeal and he looks to the future with confidence.'

Verses 1–6 are a cry for help, ending with a verse which admits that his sufferings are partly due to his own sins.

Verses 7–12 show his belief that he suffers in God's cause. In spite of his fasting and wearing sackcloth, he has become a byword to many, and even the drunkards mock at him.

Verses 13–19 are a further prayer for deliverance. Verse 18 is the heart of his cry for help: 'Do not hide your face from your servant for I am in trouble. O be swift to answer me!'

Verses 20–23 tell more about his sufferings, the insults and taunts that are heaped upon him, no one to have pity on him. His enemies even try to poison his food.

Verses 24–30 are a prayer that God should pour out his anger upon these enemies, even that he should never forgive them, but blot them out from the book of the living. The ASB suggests that these bitter verses be left out in public worship.

Verses 31–38 show that in all his sufferings he still trusts in God both for himself and for Israel. He knows that his offering of trust is more acceptable than any of the prescribed sacrifices. So, he praises God in this song and gives glory to God with thanksgiving.

The Jewish commentator whose summary was quoted in the beginning of this meditation suggests that the writer of this psalm was Jeremiah. A Christian scholar supports this: 'This psalm should be read throughout with Jeremiah in mind; whether he wrote it or not, his history gives the key to its meaning' (Professor Davison).

70   Cry for help

This psalm is a repetition of psalm 40.17–22 with one or two small changes. The writer is in urgent need and begs God to make haste. His faith is in God as deliverer and helper, and he appeals to him again not to delay.

71   In old age

Verses 9 and 18 make it clear that this psalm was written or sung by an old man, grey headed and failing in vigour, whose trust is still in God. Some scholars think that the speaker may have been David. Others think of Jeremiah. The first three verses speak of his trust in God, who is still his high rock on which he can stand secure and also his stronghold. Verses 4–13 are his prayer for deliverance by God on whom he has leaned from his earliest days. He prays: 'Cast me not away in the time of old age, nor forsake me when my strength fails'. His enemies gather round him and mock him saying that God has forsaken him, and therefore he will be an easy prey to their plotting. He prays that they will be put to shame and disgraced.

In verses 14–16, he declares his hope in God, and his resolve to speak of God's saving love, though he knows that he can never do justice to it.

In verses 17–20, he tells of the lessons he has learnt from his long life. He has gone through many bitter troubles, but God has raised him up and renewed his strength. There is none like God.

In the remaining four verses he expresses his trust that God will bless him beyond his former greatness. So he will praise God upon the lute and harp in joyful song, rejoicing that those who seek to do him harm are being shamed and disgraced.

There is a note of tenderness about this psalm, and of quiet confidence that God, who has blessed him through his long years, will also bless him in the years that are left.

72   A prayer for the nation's ruler

The heading to this psalm says that it is a psalm of Solomon, who prayed for wisdom to rule God's people well (1 Kings 3.5–9). In verses 1–7, the ideal king is described: one who judges the people rightly, with fairness for the poor of the land, rescuing the needy, restraining oppressors, bringing prosperity in a long reign of peace.

Verses 8−14 pray for the extension of his rule to all peoples from sea to sea, from the Euphrates to the ends of the then known world. Bedouin tribes who normally resist any control shall obey him. May he pity the helpless and needy, and value the lives of all his subjects.

In verses 15−19, the psalmist prays for the king personally, asking for long life, riches and prosperity, with corn growing even on the mountain tops, with ears as bursting as the famed grain of Lebanon, with every field thick with sheaves. May his name be honoured for ever, and let all nations call him blessed!

The last two verses of doxology are not part of the psalm, but praise to God at the end of the second book of the Psalter. May God's holy name be blessed for ever and the whole earth be filled with his glory! To this final prayer of praise the congregation responds 'Amen! Amen!' May all countries have such just and good rulers! Amen. Amen.

A note is appended at the end of this psalm: The prayers of David the son of Jesse are ended.

73 A perplexing problem

This psalm, like psalm 37, deals with the problem of the apparent prosperity of wicked people and the suffering of people who trust in God, and try to live according to his commandments. The first two verses tell of the conclusion he came to, after a long period of doubt when he came near to breakdown.

Verses 3−11 describe the prosperity of the wicked.

They are hale and hearty, they seem to be free of misfortunes that come to others, they have all that the heart could wish for, yet they are proud and boastful, frequently indulging in violence, they are envious of others, their conversation is full of mockery, malice, slander and blasphemy. Their lives have a corrupting influence and others follow their evil example. They think that the Most High has no knowledge of all that is going on.

In verses 12−16, the psalmist reflects on all this, and even wonders if there is any advantage in having kept his hands unstained by misdeeds and his heart morally clean. He admits to being baffled. Yet he has not spoken of his doubts publicly, lest he should undermine the faith of other believers.

His bafflement continues until he goes into the quietness of the Temple, and, as he reflects there, all becomes plain, and he sees the ultimate fate of the wicked. God sets them in slippery places, they lose their foothold and perish in terror. God rouses himself and reveals his judgment on their way of life. Their prosperity now is like a dream, it vanishes on waking (vv.18−20).

As he looks back he realizes that he was mistaken and had become little better than an animal, acting in the grip of his embittered feelings (vv.21−22).

The last six verses of the psalm speak of the return of trust in God. He is now sure that he has not been abandoned by God, as he had imagined. He now trusts that God will guide him to glory. Verses 25 and 26 constitute one of the loveliest gems of spirituality in the whole of the Old Testament: 'Whom have I in heaven but you? and there is no one upon earth that I desire in comparison with you. Though my flesh and heart fail me: you O God are my portion for ever.'

Here is a text to remember when puzzled and despondent, especially when we bear in mind that neither the

man who wrote it nor his contemporaries had any idea
of life after death nor of the possibility that God could
forgive evil doers. The last verse of his poem can be
personalized to each Christian believer:

'It is good for me to draw near to God: I have made
the Lord God my refuge and I will tell of all that you
have done.'

74   Urgent appeal

Jerusalem has been destroyed. The Temple has been
desecrated and is in ruins. People feel not only forsaken
by God, but rejected by Him in fierce anger. Opinions
differ as to when the psalm was written, some thinking it
refers to the destruction by Nebuchadnezzar in 586 BC,
and 2 Kings 25.9 would seem to support this view.
Others think it refers to the Syrian invasion, which led to
the Maccabean revolt in the second century, and this
may be supported by the mention of all the holy places
(e.g. synagogues) being burnt down.

Verses 1–3 are an appeal to God to remember that
Israel is his own possession whom he redeemed from
Egypt, and Jerusalem, where his presence was recognized. He is urged to go and inspect the ruins and to
rouse himself to come to the rescue.

In verses 4–11 the havoc in the Temple is described,
axes and hammers have damaged the sacred carving,
fires have been set alight, foreign banners erected, holy
places throughout the land destroyed. Perhaps worst of
all, there is no prophet left to comfort the people. The
despairing cry everywhere is 'How long? how long?' It
seems as if God has withdrawn his right hand, the
symbol of his power.

The writer never doubts the power of God, and in verses 12−17 remembers some of the mighty acts of God in the past, mentioning the crossing of the Red Sea, as if God had split it in two, to enable them to pass over on dry foot. The power of Egypt was crushed, symbolized as Leviathan the seven-headed monster. In the desert, rocks were split open to discover springs of water. It seemed as if ever-flowing rivers were dried up, in contrast to the wadis that dry up in summer. God has created sun and moon, the seasons of the year, and has set natural boundaries between nations, rivers and mountain ranges.

With his trust in God somewhat re-kindled by these memories of the past, he resumes his prayer to God to show his power. He feels that the whole earth is full of darkness and violence and appeals to God to arise and act, and so retrieve his reputation among the nations, putting a stop to their unending taunts and cruelties.

75 National thanksgiving

This psalm comes as a relief after all the lament and gloom of the last one. It is a song of thankfulness for deliverance from danger: Israel can add another saving act to all the wonders of the past (v.1).

In verses 2−5, God is the speaker, proclaiming that he acts at his own appointed time, upholding the moral order in the world, when human society is on the point of collapse. He is the judge who rules in justice, and brings down his arrogant. He fills his cup with retribution and the nations are made to drain it to the dregs (vv.6−10).

In the last two verses the psalmist sings praises for the triumph of righteousness and resolves to glorify God for

93

ever. He himself will be ready to break the aggression of the wicked and to strengthen and uplift the righteous.

We who meditate on this psalm today are sad at the decay of moral standards, and we pray to the God of righteousness to show us how we can help restore those fallen values.

76 The triumph of God

This psalm like many others in the Psalter is a glorification of God for the defeat of Israel's enemies, probably Sennacherib's invasion and the siege of Jerusalem (2 Kings 18.13, 19.35–36). As a result of this victory, God's renown has been magnified throughout Judah, especially in Jerusalem. The enemy's fierce arrows, shield and sword and all his weapons of war have been destroyed. The bodies of his most valiant troops litter the ground, sleeping the sleep of death. When God is really angry, none can stand before him, but flee in terror. The defeat of the invading army is a sentence of God's judgment, the very earth is awestruck.

So the wrath of man, exemplified by attacks upon the weaker neighbours, like Assyria's attack on Israel, is turned to praise for his amazing victory. The psalmist calls for the vows made in danger to be paid in the time of victory. For God has made himself to be feared among all the nations through this defeat of such a powerful monarch as Sennacherib.

77 Troubled questions

The writer of this psalm calls out to God in deep distress. Day and night he pours out his soul but receives no comfort. His spirit is overwhelmed with trouble and, though his thoughts turn to God, he continues his disturbed groanings (vv.1–3).

He has no strength to flee, he cannot sleep. A number of troubled questions arise in his mind: has God cast his people off, is his mercy clean gone, his promises forgotten, has his right hand lost all its strength? (vv.4–10).

In his search for answers to these troubling questions, he reviews Israel's past history, God's mighty acts making known his power among the nations. His wavering faith is revived in his declaration 'Your way (with Israel) O God is holy: who is so great a God as our God? You are the God that works wonders' (vv.11–15).

Particularly, the psalmist remembers God's wonderful acts at the Red Sea. The threatening waters were personified, God's voice was heard in the whirlwind and thunder, flashes of lightning lit up the landscape, the earth seemed to shudder. God's way was upon the sea, and his actions so quick that his footsteps could not be traced.

Verse 20 sums up what God was doing – he himself was guiding his people on their journey, through the leadership of Moses and Aaron. The ending seems abrupt; evidently it was a convincing answer to the psalmist's questions.

78   The lessons of history

This psalm is a survey of Israel's history from their time in Egypt to the reign of David. The fate of the Northern Kingdom is emphasized, from which it may be concluded that the poem was addressed as a warning to Judah after the ten tribes had been taken off into exile. In verse 67 there is a reference to the Temple on Mount Zion, which is evidence that the psalm was composed before the Babylonian captivity. The psalm is divided into seven sections:

Verses 1—8 describe its theme and purpose, that future generations might know of the wonderful doings of God, put their trust in him and obey his commandments. Each generation is to pass on the story to the next.

Verses 9—15 are about Israel in Egypt, opening with a criticism of the tribe of Ephraim, who are said to have gone ahead in the exodus, and later to have deserted in a critical battle. God's blessings in Goshen are remembered, then the crossing of the Red Sea, with a cloud by day and a fiery cloud by night to guide them, with streams from the sub-terranean stores of water to refresh them on the journey.

Verses 16—30 describe the people's grumbling in the desert, their doubts whether God could provide sufficient food, 'they put no trust in God, nor would they believe his power to save' (v.21), even though manna fell like seeds, so that they were supplied with corn from heaven, with flocks of wild birds providing meat.

Verses 31—38 accuse Israel of never being true to the covenant, yet in trouble they turned to God, who in his mercy remembered that they were mortal and short-lived.

Verses 39—54 recall further remembrances of God's mercies in the past, mentioning the plagues suffered by the Egyptians, whereas he guided his own people safely, and brought them to his holy land and settled them there.

Verses 55—62 describe Israel's continued disobedience and the disasters which resulted. Young men were killed and even priests fell in battle, many widows were left in mourning and hardship.

Verses 63—70 tell how God came to their rescue, and

chose the tribe of Judah, and the hill of Zion 'which He loved'. The climax of it all was the call of David to rule and shepherd them, and to care for their welfare. The psalmist's survey of history is both a message of warning, and a promise of blessing which will result from obedience.

79   Lamentation

This psalm is a lament over the destruction of Jerusalem and the Temple by the Babylonians. It has similarities with the Book of Lamentations ascribed to the prophet Jeremiah.

Verses 1–4 describe the disaster: the Temple has been desecrated and destroyed, the city is little better than a heap of stones, dead bodies lie unburied, neighbouring nations make a laughing stock of God's inheritance.

In verses 5–9 the writer puts the catastrophes down to God's anger, and prays that it may be vented upon the heathen nations instead. He realizes, however, that Israel has sinned in the past, and prays that God will hasten to have compassion on their terrible plight.

He then appeals to God for help (vv.9–12), pleading that God's honour is compromised by his failure to come to the rescue of Israel who claim to be his chosen people. He goes on to pray for those who have been taken prisoner, many of whom may be in danger of execution. Finally, he hopes that God will inflict seven times as much suffering on the victors as they have inflicted upon the inhabitants of Jerusalem.

It looks as if the outpouring of the writer's heart, in sorrow for Jerusalem, in anger against its destroyers, and in complaint to God, has brought him some relief, for in verse 13 he continues to think of himself, and the nation, as God's people ready to praise him when he comes to their help.

80 Prayer for restoration

The occasion of this psalm could also be the Babylonian captivity or possibly the earlier Assyrian captivity, in which case it would be a prayer of a psalmist in Judah for the ten tribes of the north as well.

He addresses God as the Shepherd of Israel, and pictures him enthroned in glory above the cherubim, who worship in his presence and are represented as guardians of the Ark in the Holy of Holies. The theme of the psalm is expressed in verse 3:

> Restore us again, O Lord of hosts:
> Show us the light of your countenance
> and we shall be saved.

This is a prayer which is repeated in verses 7 and 19.

This psalmist, like many others, puts down the nation's plight to God's anger, and asks how long it is to continue (vv.4–7).

He then speaks of Israel as a vine, brought by God out of Egypt and planted in the new land, where it becomes a great vine, spreading over the hills to the Mediterranean on the west, and the great river Euphrates on the east. Now the fences are broken down, wild boar root it up, passers by steal its grapes. The only hope is that God will pity its unhappy state and turn to it in mercy (vv.8–14).

The psalmist turns to prayer again, asking that God will once more care for the vine which was so flourishing, so that it is no longer cut down and used for fuel. Once again God's power will rest on its leaders, and the nation must no longer turn away from God, but acknowledge its allegiance and dependence. So he concludes with his prayer refrain: 'Restore us again, O Lord of hosts'.

Bible lovers, meditating on this psalm, will remember the prophet's song in Isaiah 5 which depicts God's love for his vineyard and the divine warning that he will leave it to a similar fate if it persists in bearing wild grapes, namely injustice and bloodshed.

The Christian will remember the graphic parable of Jesus in Matt. 21.33–41, and rather more gratefully the description of his relationship with his disciples in John 15.1–7: 'I am the true vine, and my Father is the vinedresser. Every branch of mine that bears no fruit he takes away, and every branch that does bear fruit he prunes that it may bear more fruit . . . Abide in me, and I in you.'

81 A festival song

Jewish tradition connects this psalm with the harvest festival of Tabernacles in the seventh month of the year. The celebration is to be accompanied by music – drums, lutes and harps, and finally the blowing of the ram's horn (shofar). All this was commanded by God, when Israel came out of Egypt (vv.1–5).

The psalmist says that he (or possibly Israel) had then heard a voice not previously known, but recognized as God's voice, telling of his own saving acts and warning the people against the worship of any other gods, the first commandment of the Decalogue in fact, promising 'open wide your mouth and I will fill it' (vv.6–10), reminding the reader of an earlier psalm with God's invitation 'O taste and see that the Lord is good' (34.8).

In verses 11–16 the words accepted as God's words continue accusing Israel of disobedience, resulting in their being left to go their own way. The oracle from God continues sadly, 'If only my people would listen, if Israel would but walk in my ways, I would soon put down their enemies'. Those who hate the Lord would always be punished. On the other hand, if Israel would obey the divine commands 'I would feed you with the finest wheat, and satisfy you with honey out of the rocks', a reference to the promises of Deut. 32.13–14.

The believer meditating on this psalm can hardly miss its lesson: 'Only if I obey God and keep his commandments can I expect his protection and blessing'.

82 Judges judged

The Torah, the divine Law, worked out in such detail in the so-called five books of Moses, places great emphasis on the need of just judges, an emphasis also seen in Isa. 3.14–15.

In verses 1–4 the writer asserts that God is the supreme judge, the judge of judges. He pictures a heavenly assize in which judges are accused of favouring the rich and powerful to the neglect of the poor and needy.

In verses 5–7 we get God's summing up against unjust judges: they are quite unfitted for their sacred duty, both morally and intellectually their minds are darkened and they do not understand the principles of just judgment. When the cause of justice is so often corrupted, human society is undermined. So he says that though they are godlike beings who should conform to God's will, they shall come under God's judgment and die like ordinary men.

The psalmist's final appeal to God is to arise and judge the whole earth, for all nations are his possession and he, therefore, has the right to judge them.

Anyone who has lived in Israel for some years is struck by the integrity and courageous judgments of the judges of the high court, though sometimes it must be admitted that if the party in power do not get the verdicts they want, they may take legislative action to alter the law. It should also be said that other legislatures have been known to do the same thing.

83 Unholy alliance

This psalm is a prayer for God's judgment and punishment of the nations who have combined against Israel. Faced with an overpowering military force, the psalmist invokes God's intervention on their behalf, and prays that he will do to these attacking nations what he has done to Israel's enemies in the past. The occasion is not clearly stated, but it may be the alliance of nations against Jehoshaphat, described in 2 Chron. 25, when the king and Judah 'assembled to seek help from the Lord; from all the cities of Judah they came to seek the Lord'.

Verses 1–5 describe this time of great danger. The enemies meet together to work out a plan of attack. The assembling troops are so numerous that an uproar is created. The psalmist assumes that an attack on Israel is an attack on God, but in the early stages, at least, God seems silent and inactive.

In verses 6–9, the nations taking part in this alliance against Israel are enumerated. From the south come the Edomites, like Ammon and Amalek, Israel's traditional enemies. Gebal comes from the north, Phistia and Tyre from the Mediterranean coast. Most threatening of all is

Assyria, which has already destroyed the Northern Kingdom.

The psalmist prays for the defeat of this combination of enemies, instancing the overthrow in the past of the kings of Midian. He asks that these foes may be like chaff, driven by the wind or like the even lighter thistledown. Let them be like trees and brush in a forest fire, let them be terrified by God's hurricane wind. May they be covered with shame, disgraced for ever and perish completely!

In spite of these bitter imprecations, the psalmist hopes that they may come to know God and obey his will. As Rabbi Cohen concludes: 'Not in vindictiveness is their destruction prayed for, but to demonstrate that God's rule is supreme in the world'.

84   Joy in communion with God

The writer of this psalm speaks of his great love for communion with God, which he experiences in the Temple. He has evidently been away for some considerable time and now recounts his happiness in being back once more in the sacred courts. He likens his joy in coming home to the Temple as a bird returning to its nest.

As this pilgrim comes in sight of the Temple his soul remembers how long he has been away and he exclaims 'How lovely!' He can think of no greater happiness than of ministering there and joining in the worship of the sanctuary.

In verses 5–7, he speaks of the longing in his heart that has brought him home. On his journey back, he has passed through a grove of balsam trees which manage to thrive in the driest valley. The man who trusts in God, he says, will find springs of water from which he will refresh both his physical thirst and his longing for God. All such will go from strength to strength, without becoming exhausted.

Arrived in the Temple he offers his prayer, which includes intercession for the king who rules over Israel. Turning again to his own happiness, he says that even one day in the holy courts is better than a thousand elsewhere. Even to stand in the approach to the Temple is better than living permanently in regions where godless people also live. God himself is a rampart to keep out enemies, a shield against all arrows. He will not withhold blessing from those who live innocent lives (vv.8–11).

He concludes with words of trust and worship: 'O Lord God of hosts', hosts meaning the shining ones, the angels and saints, the perfected ones who stand in his presence, confident that he too is blessed by God when he puts his trust in him.

Christians studying this psalm will remember the aged priest Simeon and the prophetess Anna, who were constantly in the Temple and were overjoyed when one day the baby Jesus was brought to be presented to the Lord. They will remember too this psalmist's confidence that however dry and tiring the journey through life, even to think of God will open up springs to refresh the heart.

There is no clue in the psalm to the identity of the writer, but all down the ages religious souls have been grateful for his song, and have echoed his words in their hearts.

85   Promise of blessings

The writer of this psalm, like the writer of the previous one, had come through troubled times. He may have been an exile who had returned to his homeland from

Babylon. He feels that God has restored the fortunes of his people, has turned away from his fierce anger, and forgiven Israel's sin (vv.1–3).

As he prays for restoration, he may not feel too sure that the nation will continue penitent and faithful, for he asks 'Will you be displeased with us for ever? Will you not give us life again?' The fact that he asks such questions shows his personal hope. His prayer is 'Show us your mercy O Lord, and grant us your salvation', which both the BCP and the ASB, adopt as versicle and response in the suffrages which follow the Lord's Prayer in Morning and Evening Prayer (vv.5–7).

He then resolves to listen to what God will say in answer to his prayer, and the remainder of the psalm is about what God wills for his people if their hearts are constantly turned to him: his presence will shine in their land; when righteous conduct is practised, the land will receive the blessing of mercy. Righteousness and peace are so intimately connected that they are pictured as kissing each other; when seeds of goodness are planted there is always a harvest of blessing. In a few words – righteousness will pave the way for him to tread.

God's will is right conduct, his promise is a peaceful and happy nation.

86   Trust in trouble

This psalm, said to be a psalm of David, is the only one so headed in Book Three of the psalms. The writer is in great trouble and depression, for he prays that he may be made glad. He believes that God is good and forgiving, continuously kind to all who call upon him (vv.1–5).

The psalmist is confident that God will hear and

answer him, for there is no one like God. His hope is that all nations shall be united under God's sovreignty, for he alone is God (vv.6–10).

Then he prays for God's guidance and to be shown the way of the Lord, when he will thank him with all his heart, for God will have saved him from death (vv.11–13).

The last four verses are a prayer for protection from violent men. This appeal is almost identical with psalm 54–5. He quotes also Exod. 34.6, a divine word heard by Moses, assuring him of compassion, mercy and truth. So he prays for strength and asks from him a sign, a manifestation which will vindicate him and prove to his enemies that it is God who has rescued him.

He ends his prayer with words of faith, acknowledging gratefully that it is God who is his helper and comforter.

87 Universal birthplace, home and centre

This is a most interesting and remarkable psalm, which comes refreshingly after so many poems of narrow nationalism, so many invocations of God to punish, and even destroy, those nations which are hostile to Israel.

The first two verses speak of Zion, founded by God, on a hill regarded as holy even before it became David's capital, even before the Temple was built there. It is the City of God, loved by him more than any other place in Israel and, in the mind of the writer, more than any other place on earth. He somehow knows that in the future, glorious things shall be spoken of her.

He goes on to think of places, near and far, where his kinsmen have gone to live, even in Egypt and Babylon, many of whom were born in those places. Many had the good fortune to be born in Zion itself. God has indeed both founded the city and been responsible for its growth and fame.

It could be that the psalmist was thinking in the first place of Jews settled in many other countries: they are all citizens, their children are citizens too. Jerusalem is their spiritual birthplace and home (vv.3–4).

In verse 5 the psalmist pictures God writing up his register of the nations, and including them, though he notes the actual physical birthplace of each. This possible interpretation is strengthened by a verse from the previous psalm (86.12): 'All the nations you have made shall come and worship before you: O Lord they shall glorify your name'.

So Zion is thought of as the birthplace of all; all have a right to come there as their home. We can be grateful to the final editor of the Book of Psalms, for putting these psalms 86 and 87 together.

So Zion is the world centre. The writer of the Book of Revelation gives us a vision of God's new Jerusalem, beautiful with every lovely jewel he can think of, the nations and their rulers streaming into it, with its gates eternally open. The writer of the Epistle to the Hebrews speaks of Jerusalem as 'that is above, the Mother of us all'.

The writer of our psalm, in his last verse, speaks of great rejoicing in the mother city of God, calling to singers to praise God, and dancers to weave a pattern of universal significance and relationship. One regrets, however, the disapperance of the BCP theme of both singers and dancers, 'All my fresh springs shall be in Thee'. Hebrew scholars tell us that the exact meaning of this verse is obscure. The spiritual message that all our happiness and blessedness are in God and his Eternal City, is one to be thankful for.

88 Not a glimmer of hope

This psalm is quite the most gloomy one in the whole of the Psalter. The writer speaks out of intense personal suffering. He prays for relief, but without much hope that relief will come. Yet the fact that he prays is a sign of some faith, as is also the first words of his prayer 'O Lord my God'.

In verses 1–9, he tells of his miserable state. He is near to death, imprisoned in the lowest pit of despair, forsaken by his friends, feeling that God's anger is on him.

In verses 10–13, he cries to God to come to his help before it is too late, pleading that the dead cannot praise him, for it is a land of complete forgetfulness.

In verses 14–19, in spite of his gloom and despair, he still persists in prayer, yet also feeling that God's anger has overwhelmed him.

Some commentators think that there must have been a lost ending to this psalm, for in other psalms of a similar character, prayer has resulted in a sense of trust and encouragement. The Christian may feel critical of this poor sufferer, but we who live in the era of the New Testament have the assurance of God's inexhaustible grace and the gospel news of resurrection, and of the revelation of Jesus the Christ that God is not a God of anger and punishment, but one of saving love.

89 An urgent prayer in national adversity

This psalm is a prayer for the renewal of God's mercies in a time of national trouble and defeat. The circumstances described in the second half of the psalm suggest that it was written after the downfall of the nation brought about by the Babylonians. There are two main divisions in it, verses 1–38 describing the past and particularly God's covenant with David, and verses 39–53 speaking of the unhappy present and the overthrow of the nation. The writer is perplexed at the promises made to David, notably verse 4, 'I will establish your line for ever, and build up your throne for all generations'. He contrasts this promise with the disastrous happenings culminating in verse 45: 'You have brought his lustre to an end, You have cast this throne to the ground'.

In verses 6–18, God's greatness is acknowledged, none can compare with him, he controls the turbulent sea, he defeated Egypt. He is the creator of the earth and the heavens, he rules the world from one end to the other. He is worshipped in the heavenly hosts, righteousness and justice, loving kindness and mercy mark his rule: Israel is God's people.

In verses 19–38, God himself speaks of the covenant with David, a young man chosen out of the people, a great and successful warrior, who will rule from the Western Sea (the Mediterranean) to the great rivers of Mesopotamia, who will call God his Father and be his first-born son. The psalmist pictures God warning the nation that if they forsake his Law he will punish them, but he will not break his covenant with David. His throne and royal line will endure for ever.

A break comes with verse 39 and the psalmist accuses God of anger against his anointed one, breaking down his defences and inflicting rejection and defeat, so that all the king's enemies rejoice and taunt him.

The last six verses are an appeal to God for mercy, asking if he has created man for nothing, and how long his anger is to continue, with an implicit prayer that he will restore his loving kindness of the past, and be faithful to the vow made to David. There is an almost personal note in this appeal, which speaks of the writer's grief in all that is happening. 'Remember O Lord, remember!'

Verse 53 is not part of the original psalm; it is a doxology ending this Third Book of the Psalms, blessing God forever, the editor adding his repeated Amen, praying 'So be it!' So may it always be!

90 Man is mortal

In the headings of the various biblical versions of the psalms, this psalm is ascribed to 'Moses, the man of God'. In his final blessing to the twelve tribes, Moses assures them: 'The eternal God is your dwelling place, and underneath are the everlasting arms' (Deut. 33.27). This is the gospel-like message of psalm 90, after its writer speaks at length about the mortality of man. The psalm falls into three clear sections:

Verses 1–6: Man's short life is contrasted with God's eternity, before time was and after time shall cease to be.

Verses 7–10: In the opinion of the psalmist, the troubles of man's short life are due to God's anger because of man's sin.

Verses 11–17: A prayer for wisdom to realize the brevity of life and to live in such a way that will result in a restoration of God's favour. God's eternity existed before ever the mountains appeared, they being regarded as the most solid and permanent features in the created world.

With man, time passes very quickly especially in the night when he sleeps. With God time does not count; one thousand years to him is but yesterday, whereas our years pass away quickly like a sigh (v.9), or as the BCP says, like a tale that is told and quickly forgotten. Many people live to three score years and ten; some are so

109

strong that they live a further ten years. But at the longest, human life is very short and old age becomes wearisome. We die and our bodies become particles of dust. All this is due to sin, and in God's presence our most secret sins are known.

So the psalmist prays for a return of God's mercy, asking that we may have as much gladness in the future as we have had sadness in the past. He goes on to pray that God's working may be made plain to us who live now and that our children may see glorious results (v.16). Finally, he asks that God will prosper our daily tasks and that his gracious favour may rest upon us.

Isaac Watts' well-known hymn 'O God, our help in ages past' is based on this psalm. It has a decidedly more hopeful note about it, and its last line speaks of God as our eternal home. That is how it should be, for he wrote it well over two thousand years later than the psalmist, and after seventeen hundred years of the Easter gospel.

91   God our protector

After the rather gloomy reflections upon human life in the preceding psalm, this psalm expresses a quieter and more confident trust in God's protection. Some scholars have thought that it may have been written by the same writer, presenting, as it were, the other side of the coin. If this is not so, it may have been the inspired thought of the final editor of the book of the Psalms to place it next to psalm 90 and so add a compensating view of human life.

Three speakers seem to take part in it: the first addressing God as his shelter, refuge and fortress, and speaking from the happy experience of living so close to him that no danger can reach him (vv.1–2).

A second voice speaks of God's protection from every kind of evil – attack in the night, arrows shot at him during the day, snares set by the hunter, a noxious pestilence that kills many, a curse set upon him by a malicious enemy. In all of these he will be safe under the motherly wings of God. One may wonder about the exact meaning of verse 7, 'A thousand shall fall beside you, and ten thousand at your right hand, but you it shall not touch'. Perhaps the thousands refer to arrows rather than fellow men. The second speaker thinks of God commanding his angels to guard the writer in all his ways, and to bear him up in their hands lest he should dash his foot against a stone, a text on which Jesus meditated during the forty days in the Jericho country-side after his baptism.

This section (vv.3–13) ends with the assurance that God will defend those who trust him against the strongest lions in their prime or the most poisonous snakes that lurk in his path.

In the last three verses of the psalm God himself is the speaker, promising those who cling to him in love safety beyond the reach of any enemies, immediate answers to every prayer for help, with a long and satisfying life, well worth living, and, above all, the full joy of salvation.

92 A sabbath hymn

According to Jewish tradition and symbolic expression this psalm was sung by Adam on the first sabbath of creation. The writer realizes that he lives in a world where often the wicked seem to prosper, causing anxiety and injury to good people. He lifts his eyes from the physical and material world with its worries and trials to the world which is always bright with the radiant glory

111

of God. This enables him to sing praises to God, even though the ungodly are not yet defeated. The psalmists always look forward to the triumph of God, often speaking of it as already present.

Verses 1–3: Thanksgiving to God, whose love is remembered morning and evening, and accompanied on the harp.

Verses 4–5: The great works of God in the past fill the heart with joy. In verse 5 God's way of working in the universe, in allowing the wicked to triumph temporally, is said to be very deep, beyond man's comprehension, a thought similar to that of Isaiah 55.8: 'For my thoughts are not your thoughts, neither are your ways my ways'. Brutish and foolish men do not realize that their prosperity will be short-lived.

Verses 6–11: The writer is confident that his strength will more than equal that of enemies comparable to wild bulls. He feels his spirit uplifted, as if anointed with sacramental oil.

Verses 12–15: The righteous will flourish like a palm tree in desert soil, and be as long-lived as a cedar in Lebanon. Even in old age they will be full of sap and enterprise, putting out great branches. For they are planted in God's house, and he is the rock of their faith.

The writer has written his hymn for recital in the Temple, and it is based on his own experience.

93   King of the universe

This is the first of a short series of psalms (93–100) often spoken of as 'royal psalms'. Commentators think that they began at the return from exile in Babylon, marking the beginning of a new era after a period when many feared that God had abdicated. Now people saw him as actively taking charge again, not only of Israel but of the whole universe. The future is in his hands; so this psalm and those that follow it have a messianic interpretation of world-wide reform.

The first three verses proclaim that the Lord has been enthroned and has put on the royal robes of coronation. He is determined to uphold righteousness. The psalmist, looking back on countless ages, sees once more God's creation of the world, still firm and stable. God has been ruling the world from the beginning of time.

In verses 4–5, the writer thinks of the recent happenings as a tidal wave, accompanied by great thunderings, great waves of the sea breaking upon the shore. The Lord is mightier than these.

In the final verse, the psalmist expresses to God his conviction that his moral laws are 'very sure', unshakeable and unchanging. God's holiness is revealed 'in your house' which refers not only to the Temple and Zion, but also to the universe as a whole.

This psalm is recited every Friday evening before the sabbath. It is like a short creed of Israel's faith, a glad acknowledgment of his universal sovereignty. Used in this way over many centuries, it must generate a faith that God can control any storms that may come in the future, as he has done in stormy times in the past.

94 Judge of all

According to this psalmist, the whole world is in moral chaos, justice is denied to those who need it. So he appeals to God, the supreme judge, to deal with the situation (vv. 1–2).

In verses 3–7 he describes the oppressors, who crush the people, murdering widows and orphans and aliens alike, boasting that God does not see what is going on.

In the next four verses, the psalmist tells how foolish

the unrighteous are. Most certainly, he says, God, creator of the eye, sees everything. He who created the ear hears all that is said. He knows even the thoughts of everyone's heart.

Then the writer speaks of the blessings of the righteous. God will train and teach him, never forsake him. The true of heart shall be vindicated (vv.12–15).

He goes on to speak of his own experience. There have been times when his foot has slipped: God's mercy held him up. He has had his doubts: God's comfort has assured and delighted him (vv.16–19).

Injustice shall be exposed, unjust rulers judged and silenced. He puts all his trust in God, a veritable rock, refuge and stronghold. Blessed be God!

95 Venite – O come and worship

The first two verses are a call to worship, to shout for joy, to gaze at God with thankfulness, to join in singing joyful psalms.

For, says the psalmist, he is the Supreme Creator, a great king above all the powers of the earth, so great that he holds the whole world in his hand (vv.3–5).

So we bow down in worship, we kneel in reverence. He is our God, we are his people. He is our shepherd, we are his sheep (vv.6–7).

Then the psalmist utters a solemn warning, reminding his hearers how their fathers doubted God's power to supply their needs in the wilderness, as they journeyed to the promised land. He speaks of God as loathing that generation, because they did not know his ways. He pleads longingly 'If only you would hear God's voice', all would be well. If not, you will never find rest in the land of God's promise.

114

This psalm is directed to be sung at the beginning of the sabbath. In the BCP and the ASB it is to be said or sung at the opening of each day's morning prayer – 'O come, let us worship!'

96 Open invitation

The preceding psalm was a call to Israel to worship God. This psalm is a call to all nature and all nations to worship him. In 1 Chron. 16.23–33, this psalm is reproduced almost verbatim. In that context, it is said to have been composed by David when he brought the Ark to Jerusalem, but most scholars are agreed that it is post-exilic and was incorporated by the writer of Chronicles, and not the other way round.

It claims to be a new song of praise to God as the Lord of the whole earth and for his self-revelation in his wonderful deeds (vv.1–3). He is worthy to be praised and revered above the gods worshipped by the nations. They are nothing but idols, things of nought without reality (vv.4–6).

All nations are invited to join Israel in the courts of the Temple. Gentiles are actually invited in, and to worship him in awe, acknowledging the beauty of his holiness (vv.7–9).

The nations are told that he is the creator and just judge of all, so the earth may rejoice, the heavens be glad, and the seas shout his praise; the countryside and trees of the forest will also join in the choir.

The psalmist's message is that God comes, yes he comes, to rule the earth with righteousness and its peoples with truth. His coming is an occasion for universal gladness (vv.10–13).

97　God the universal king

This psalm carries on the theme of psalm 96, fathering phrases from other psalms in a mosaic of praise. God is manifested as king, so the earth may rejoice, and the many coastlands and islands of the Mediterranean join in his worship. His coming is marked by clouds and darkness, by peals of thunder and flashes of lightning. Mountains, regarded as the most firm and solid part of the world, dissolve like wax before him. The heavens proclaim his righteousness and all nations see his glory (vv.1–6).

His coming has its effect on idolaters, all the powers worshipped as gods bow down before him, Jerusalem rejoices at the news and all the little towns of Judah are overjoyed. The psalmist addresses God as most high over the whole world, over everything else that people worship (vv.7–10).

For God loves all that hate evil, guards the faithful believers and delivers them from the power of the godless. So, 'Light dawns for the righteous, and joy for the true of heart'. The righteous are bidden to rejoice and give thanks for this glorious revelation (vv.11–12).

98　Nature summoned to worship

This psalm is said to be a thanksgiving to God for Israel's return from exile. God's saving act was so great that all the surrounding nations knew of it. The promise in Isaiah 52.1, like this psalm, mentions God's holy arm and his powerful right hand, 'so that all the ends of the earth have seen the salvation of our God' (vv.1–3).

So the psalmist calls the whole earth to celebrate with trumpets, harps, the ram's horn and a choir of singers. The whole world and its inhabitants are invited to join, as are the great powers of nature — the waves of the sea are to clap their hands and the mountains to break into song (vv.4—8).

The last verse is a repetition of the final verse of psalm 96; both celebrate the arrival of the Lord to rule the whole earth, and fulfil his faithfulness to Israel.

99 God reigns

God is pictured as enthroned upon the cherubims, the representations of which, guard the Ark in the holy of holies. The nations are awe-struck at what has happened, for God is seen exalted high above the nations (vv.1—3).

The divine king who loves justice is now ruling over all. So the psalmist and possibly the worshippers in the Temple sing: 'O exalt the Lord our God, and fall down before his footstool, for he is holy' (vv.4—5).

In verses 6—9 God's dealings with his people in the past are remembered; Moses and Aaron 'among his priests', and Samuel the great prophet, are spoken of as praying to God, who answered them from the cloud hiding his presence. These leaders obeyed God's Law and followed his teaching. God answered them and forgave their wrong doings. So the refrain of verse 5 is repeated, calling all to bow in worship in Zion, 'his holy hill', for he is a God of holiness, and the king over all the earth.

100 Joy for all nations

This short psalm is an invitation to all the peoples of the world to join with Israel in the worship of God, to serve him gladly, with hearts full of joy in his goodness and faithfulness. He is God, he is the creator of all; we all belong to him. He is our shepherd, we are his flock.

In verse 3, we are invited to enter his gates, namely the gates of the Temple, with worshipping, grateful and blessing hearts. This invitation will remind us of Isaiah's hope that foreigners will join Israel in the worship and service of God, 'for my house shall be called a house of prayer for all peoples' (56.6—7). This text was quoted by Jesus, when his heart burned with indignation at the irreverent practices that went on in the Temple in his day.

Verse 4 supplies a reason for the joyful worship for which the psalmist calls: The Lord is good (see also Mark 10.18 'No one is good but God alone'), his loving mercy endures for ever (see psalm 136), his truth and faithfulness throughout all generations.

So we bless his holy name, the revelation to us of his nature, character and will, we defend his goodness and reputation, and we pray each day 'Hallowed be your name', by each one, by Israel, by the church, as it is revered by angels and saints in his presence.

101   A king's prayer

Some commentators think this to be the prayer of a king, in which he formulates the principles that will guide his reign.

Verses 1—3: His longing for God's presence, thought by some scholars to express David's desire for a worthy house for the Ark.

Verses 4—9: He will not associate with wicked and perverse people, but will choose righteous advisers.

Verses 10–11: He pledges himself to administer justice and to purge Jerusalem of the wicked.

Verse 3: His private life will not be tarnished by corruption and indulgence, as is the case in most Eastern courts.

Verse 7: He will not put up with slander, nor proud pretentions and arrogant hearts.

The worshipper today will know that the holy and righteous God will only dwell in the hearts of those who want to be holy and righteous, in all their dealings and relationships.

102   A psalmist in trouble

We have come to the end of the short series of 'royal psalms', and are once again with a psalmist in trouble, physical and mental, who longs to be back in Jerusalem, even in its ruined state. The heading to the psalm sums up its theme: 'A prayer of the afflicted, when he fainteth, and poureth out his complaint before the Lord'. There is an echo of the royal psalms, for his longing is for the restoration of Jerusalem, where the nations will honour God's name and see his glory (vv.12–16).

The writer opens with a verse that has become very familiar as the versicle and response that begins mattins and evensong, and is also used after many biddings to intercession. He applies it to his own day of trouble, when he fears that God has turned his face away from him.

In verses 3–11, he describes his desperate state, wasted away in some long illness, his whole body in a fever, his bones aching, and his heart, which should be a source of vitality and strength withered within him. He is restless and cannot sleep. He is melancholy as a pelican in the wilderness or as an owl amidst ruins, as mournful as a sparrow on a housetop mourning the loss of its mate.

In his sad state, taunted by enemies, he turns to God 'enthroned for ever'; his condition reminds him of his grief over Jerusalem. He pleads that a time of mercy is long overdue, he tells of his love for the city, even though it is little more than heaps of rubble. As he prays on, hope returns and he voices his faith that its restoration will bring the nations back to fear God, as well as be a matter of praise for future generations. With restoration, prisoners will be released and those about to be killed by their captors will be spared (vv.12–22).

For a moment, his thoughts turn again to his own wretched plight. He is evidently still in the prime of life, when he might well expect years of health and strength. Quickly, however, he thinks again of God's eternity, and hope and faith begin to be revived. It was God who laid the foundations of the world. The heavens and the earth will pass away, they grow old and can be discarded like a change of clothes. 'But You are the same for ever, and your years will never fail.' (v.27)

So we, your servants and our children, and their children with them, can rest secure, firmly planted, happy in your sight, your face no longer turned away but shining upon us in blessing.

103   A joyful hymn

The date of this psalm is thought by scholars to be soon after the return from exile in Babylon. In the first half of the psalm, the singular person is used, in the second it changes to the plural suggesting that, in his personal thanksgiving, the writer merges his individuality in the nation. It is one of the most joyful of all the psalms.

Verses 1—5: The psalmist calls to himself to praise God.

6—18: He praises God for his graciousness.

19—22: He speaks of God as the King of the universe.

Verse 1: He praises God for his holiness, the essence of God's nature.

He lists the benefits which God bestows, which include forgiveness of sin and healing physical ailments.

Verse 4: God saves from the grave. The psalmist did not die in captivity but was granted the happiness of returning to Zion.

Verse 5: The Hebrew is 'who satisfieth thine old age with good things; so that thy youth is renewed like the eagle'. He not only lives to a great age but retains his vitality. The eagle has been known to live to a hundred years.

Verse 7: Moses' prayer in Exod. 33.13, 'Show me thy ways'. A few verses later, Moses prays 'Show me thy glory'.

Verse 8: This recalls Exod. 34.6: 'The Lord, the Lord, a God merciful and gracious, slow to anger, and abounding in steadfast love and faithfulness'.

Verse 9: God is a righteous judge who cannot overlook sin, but he is a compassionate and merciful God.

Verses 10—12: His forgiveness is beyond measure, as high as the sky, as wide as the earth.

Verses 14—16: He remembers that we are mortal, like the grass which shoots up with the early rains, but is soon scorched by the hot wind from the desert. This passage is often quoted at funerals and contrasted in verse 17 with God's eternal mercy.

Verse 21: 'all ye his hosts' are the heavenly bodies and forces of nature.

The last four verses assert that Israel's experience of God's rule and blessing is available for other nations as well. He calls to all angels, to the host of heavenly bodies, to all the forces of nature, to people everywhere to praise and bless God. The last words of this glorious hymn of praise return to the personal worship of the opening line 'Bless the Lord, O my soul'.

104   Hymn of creation

The writer of this psalm presents to us a picture of the whole cosmos, which leads him to discern, behind all its wonders and beauties, the creative power of God. It may have been written by the same poet who wrote psalm 103, for both begin and end with the call to his own soul to praise and bless the Lord.

Verses   1–5: The greatness of God.
        6–10: The foundations of the earth.
    11–14: Springs and rain.
    15–17: Food for cattle and man.
    18–19: Trees and birds.
        20: Goats and badgers.
    21–25: Moon and sun.
    26–32: All created beings depend on God.
    33–37: The poet resolves to praise God, and prays that sinners may cease in the earth.

Dean Stanley thought that the author may have written this poem on Mount Lebanon, when the great cedars would be in near focus and the Mediterranean more distinct, yet he could see passing ships and possibly the spout of an occasional whale (vv.18, 27–28). In our age, the camera with its variety of lenses and the skill and patience of those who use it, help us to appreciate the natural world even more deeply and to marvel at the mind of the Creator.

This psalm like the first chapter of the Bible should be thought of as poetry rather than science. The writer sees God revealed in storms, winds and flashes of lightning.

Verse 34: The psalmist, meditating on creation and the wonders of nature, finds in God unfailing joy. We can be grateful to the modern camera, and to the patience and skill of photographers, who wait for hours in quiet stillness until the creatures small and great feel confident enough to go about their daily and nightly life.

Verse 35: There is a story related in the Talmud of a rabbi who prayed that lawless men should perish. His wife, overhearing him, prayed that sins should be consumed out of the earth, and then the wicked will be no more because they will have repented. 'Let evil cease' is a good prayer for all who are troubled by the sin and suffering in the world.

The psalm ends with the word 'Hallelujah', the first mention of a word of praise that is used frequently in both the worship of the Synagogue and the Church, meaning 'Praise the Lord'.

105   God's wonderful acts

The writer of this psalm looks back on God's dealings with Abraham and his descendants up to the time of their entry into the promised land. It was possibly composed on their return from exile, their second entry into the land of promise, which reminded those present of that first arrival after the forty years in the wilderness, corresponding to the seventy years of forced absence in

Babylon. So the psalmist calls to all who look to God to be joyful in heart, remembering the wonderful things that God has done (vv.1–6).

He bids his hearers remember God's covenant made with the patriarchs, a covenant made with Abraham, confirmed with Isaac and Jacob, and then to all the generations of Israel, the divine promise of a homeland. He reminds them that they were a very small nation, who had wandered homeless through one nation after another, protected by God as his own people (vv.7–11).

He recalls the famine that led the patriarch to go into Egypt in search of corn, and the divine care of Joseph, forgotten in prison but finally raised to be the chief minister after the Pharaoh (vv.16–22).

God's care and blessing were continued in Egypt where they increased and became powerful until a later Pharaoh reduced them to slavery. Then God raised up Moses and Aaron. A whole series of plagues were signs to the Egyptians and to Israel alike that Israel was under God's protecting care (vv.23–36).

This care continued during the exodus, and in the desert, when water was discovered in the rock and the manna and flocks of quails were seen as food from heaven. Hovering over them was a protecting guiding cloud by day and night (vv.37–45).

All this proved that God had been faithful to his promises to Abraham, with the implication that he would continue his faithfulness to those coming back in this second exodus, from Babylon. So the returning exiles are bidden to shout with joy, because these saving acts prove that they are still God's chosen people. The psalmist concludes by pointing out God's hidden purpose in all that is happening, that they may faithfully obey the laws and statutes of God.

It is interesting to note that verses 1–15 of this psalm have been incorporated into 1 Chron. 16.8–22, as an

124

appropriate psalm to be sung at commemorations of the great event when David brought back the Ark to Jerusalem.

106   Israel's disloyalty and God's faithfulness

Like psalm 105 this psalm is a retrospect of Israel's history showing how all through the period between leaving Egypt and arriving in the promised land, and even in later periods, they had been disobedient. Yet God had remained faithful to his covenant and had rescued and forgiven them time after time. The psalm opens with praise and declares a blessing on those who always act justly and do right. The rest of the psalm is a confession of national sins, listing seven occasions.

The first is a lack of faith at the Red Sea, when God saved them from the hand of the Egyptians, and the Israelites were only convinced when they saw the drowning of their enemies (vv.6–13).

However, they soon forgot their deliverance, and grumbled at the scarcity of food and refused to trust God (vv.14–16). They revolted against Moses and Aaron (vv.17–19). At Horeb they made and worshipped a golden calf, comparing God to a creature that eats grass. The psalmist pictures God as ready to destroy them for this blasphemous imagery, and recounts Moses' prayer to avert the divine anger (vv.20–27). At Peor they worshipped the heathen Baal, and took part in sacrifices to lifeless idols (vv.28–31). They grumbled at lack of water at Meribah, which caused Moses to speak rashly (vv.32–33). Even after entering Canaan, they offered human sacrifices unto the heathen gods of the land. As a result, they fell under the hand of their enemies. Time after time God delivered them, even when they refused to learn from past experience (vv.40–43).

In the face of all this God kept faithful to his covenant and did not withdraw his loving kindness. So the psalmist ends this sorry tale of the nation's many failures with a prayer that God will gather them from the nations where they have been scattered, so that they may return to their own land, give thanks to him and witness proudly to what he has done.

The last verse of the psalm is both a blessing of God for his continuing rescues, and also a closing doxology of book 4 of the Psalter.

The disciple meditating on this psalm finds it difficult to believe that God commanded Israel to destroy the peoples of the land and punished them for not doing so, although he can well accept that this was commonly believed. He may have heard of the mediaeval rabbi who pictured God weeping over his Egyptian children drowned in the Red Sea.

As one studies the psalm more deeply, one realizes the patience of God, his refusal to be defeated by the recalcitrance of his people whom he was training for a universal purpose. The message has to become personalized and each believer give heartfelt thanks to God as patiently, lovingly and undefeatably, he works to raise each and all to the potential of being created in the image of God, shown so clearly in his one perfect son, Jesus the universal Christ.

Julian of Norwich confirms this thought in her *Revelations of Divine Love*. She hears God saying to her:

> See! I am God: see! I am in all things: see! I do all things: see! I lift never my hands off my works, nor ever shall, without end: see! I lead all things to the end I ordained it from without beginning, by the same Might, Wisdom and Love whereby I made it. How should any thing be amiss?

Although this psalm begins a new book of the Psalter it is, in theme, the last of the series looking back in retrospect on past history. It is a call to exiles returning from the four points of the compass, who prayed to God in their distress and he came to their rescue (vv.1–3).

Some of these returning travellers got lost on the way and (many died of hunger and thirst) and were guided by God till they came to a city where they could find shelter and food. They are called to give thanks for God's mercies (vv.4–9).

Others had been in prison in dark dungeons bound with iron fetters, through their transgressions against God's laws. They tripped headlong and helpless and cried to God for help, with the result that their chains were broken and the threat of death removed. They are bidden to give thanks to him, in a similar chorus of praise (vv.10–16).

Some were foolish and so exhausted that they could hardly eat food. They, too, had the good sense to cry to God for help. They were healed and saved from sinking into the pit of death. They are urged to tell of God's goodness with shouts of joy (vv.17–22).

Others had to come back by sea and were tossed by great waves, staggering like drunken men, in terrifying storms. In answer to their prayers God calmed the storms and they were able to reach their destination in safety. They are urged to tell of their adventures to the leaders of their home towns (vv.23–32).

The psalmist then turns to God's control of the land, and tells how some fertile lands have become barren because of the wickedness of the inhabitants, like the region of Sodom and Gomorrah, now nothing more than a salt waste. On the other hand, there is land, formerly wilderness, which now is watered by springs, where the hungry can grow food and plant vineyards, where cattle can graze and the inhabitants even build a city, all due to the blessing of God (vv.33–38).

This psalm closes with the picture of God lifting the poor out of misery, and giving large and happy families. The upright rejoice at all this blessing, and the wicked are silenced, not destroyed. The wise man reflecting on this will see that God is at work in human affairs and that his loving kindness never ceases (vv.39–43). The believer in God meditating on this psalm will recognize that his will is for righteous living and human happiness.

108   God our defender

This psalm consists of two extracts from other psalms, verses 1–5 coming from psalm 57.8–12, and verses 6–13 from psalm 60.5–12.

The first part is one of thanksgiving for God's mercy on one whose heart is fixed on God, whose first thought each morning is to sing to God accompanied by lute and harp, with the intention of letting his praise be known among the nations. God's greatness and faithfulness reach to the heavens, even above them, and his glory is over all the earth.

Verses 6–13 are a prayer for help in danger, in which the psalmist hears God speaking of his care for Israel's tribes, and of the powerlessness of neighbouring enemies to harm them. However, it may seem that God has cast them off, he knows that in God's power 'we shall do valiantly' and be able to defeat all enemies.

The Christian will remember Luther's great hymn 'A safe stronghold our God is still'.

109   Relieving a bitter heart

This psalm is a prayer for vengeance on a malicious and cruel enemy, quite the fiercest in the whole Psalter. Its opening words 'O God of my praise' hardly prepare us for its vehement curses that are invoked in verses 5–19.

The writer's heart is hurt and bitter against those to whom he has given friendship and love as they repay his good with lying and evil. He implores God not to keep silent (vv.1–4).

Then there follows a shocking list of curses and merciless invectives called down on the head of a particular enemy and on his parents, wife and children, praying that their sins may be constantly remembered before God, but their names never remembered on the earth (vv.5–19).

Some Jewish commentators, as shocked as readers today, have thought that these maledictions were not uttered by the psalmist against his persecutors, but by the persecutors against the psalmist. However, this conclusion is hardly convincing. What can rightly be said is that the writer must have suffered grievously, with a burning sense of injustice.

The last six verses of the psalm suggest that the bitter outburst may have brought relief, for now he prays that God's benediction may be greater than the maledictions showered on him by the enemy in question. He can pray that all such may be covered with shame. As for himself, he is now confident in God's aid, as if God were standing at his side in vindication and support.

In one's meditation there may come the memory of the counter corrective mentioned by Jesus in the opening verses of the Sermon on the Mount, which bring blessedness and happiness, and his clear unequivocal instruction to his disciples, 'Love your enemies and pray

129

for those who persecute you, so that you may be children of your Father in heaven' (see Matt. 5.3–12, 44–45).

110 God's priest-king

The psalmist pictures God as the Lord of all, inviting the writer's own king and lord to sit in authority at God's right hand and extend his rule, until all enemies are defeated and bow in submission. The sceptre held in the royal hand in Jerusalem is a symbol and assurance of authority delegated to him by God. It has been intended by God from the day of his birth (vv.1–3).

Then comes a reference to Melchisedek, described in Genesis 14 as king of Salem and priest of God Most High, who met Abraham after he had defeated a combined army of kings and rescued Lot, his nephew, from capture. Melchisedek blessed Abraham and brought bread and wine for his refreshment, while Abraham gave him a tenth of all he had. So Melchisedek is acknowledged as a priest-king long before Moses and Aaron, and the king in question is promised that he is to be a king-priest for ever, 'after the order of Melchisedek'.

It is not easy to decide who this priest-king is. Many have thought that it must refer to David, of whom it is said that he wore the sacerdotal ephod and offered sacrifices before the Lord (2 Sam. 6.17–18). Some scholars have thought that the reference may have been to Simon Maccabee, who combined the office of King and High Priest. Still others have seen a reference to a universal priesthood, long before the covenant at Mount Sinai, when Israel became a priest-nation.

The writer of the Epistle to the Hebrews sees the

promise fulfilled in Christ, a priest for ever, after an eternal order of priesthood, through his offering of himself on the Cross for the sins of all, and who ever lives to make intercession for all who draw near to God (5.5–6, 7.23–25). The meditating Christian knows that through the Cross the love of God has been shown to the uttermost and God's unlimited forgiveness made available for all who penitently and gratefully are ready to receive it.

To come back to the psalm, there was clearly the hope and the longing for a priest who would be a king, and a king who would be a priest in heart and character, and one who would judge all nations.

The last verse pictures such a priest-and-king, who however tired and thirsty, would be refreshed and made confident by streams that he found on his way, drinking from them and finding himself restored with courage and confidence. So are all who trust God in every age.

111 God is good

This psalm opens with the call of the Levite, or precentor, to join in the service of praise. It means 'Praise ye the Lord (Jah)', familiar to Christians as the invitation to praise at the beginning of matins and evensong.

Verse 1: 'with my whole heart', completely absorbed in the worship of God, whether individually or in public worship.

The next eight verses list the wonderful works of God, especially in the history of Israel: the exodus from Egypt (v.9), the covenant which is valid for ever (vv.5 and 9), the settlement in Canaan (v.6), provision of food (v.5). All God's works are true and just, his guidance is reliable and sure (vv.7 and 8). His name is holy and awe-inspiring (v.9).

Verse 10 is echoed in Prov. 1.7 and 9.10. The fear of the Lord is the starting point for both wisdom and holiness. By 'fear' is meant reverence and awe, inspiring a life on a higher plane than mere animal existence. God's ways need study, understanding and obedience.

The last phrase echoes the opening words of the psalm, the praise of God, like the righteousness mentioned in v.3, is eternal.

The individual looking back on his life can praise God for his unchanging righteousness, mercy and guidance, and dedicate his life to the imitation of God.

112   Man too must be good

This psalm carries on the thought of psalm 111 and its first verse takes up the last verse, 'The fear of the Lord', which is not only the beginning of wisdom but also brings happiness and delight to the heart. The man who reverences God is not motivated by fear of punishment or even a sense of duty, but by joy in the imitation of God.

Verse 2: The God-fearing man will see his family and descendants enjoying this God-likeness and joy (see 25.12).

Verse 3: His unshaken righteousness will bring prosperity.

Verse 4: The light of God will shine in dark moments and enable him to become gracious, compassionate and righteous, sharing in the divine characteristics.

Verse 5: In his business affairs he will be scrupulous, ready to give a helping hand to those in need and to do so graciously and sensitively.

Verse 6: His good deeds will be gratefully remembered by his fellow men and by God.

> The best part of a good man's life
> His little unremembered acts
> Of kindness and of love.
>   (Wordsworth)

Verse 7: He will not be knocked out by misfortune or dismayed by bad news, because of his complete trust in God. The ill-will and unkind acts of others will not shake him, for he has an inner happiness which they do not.

Verse 8: He is generous in spending his money on good causes. Today, we are conscious of the needs of the old and lonely, the sick and disabled, the victims of violence, the unemployed, the hungry third world. He will be glad to assist societies like Christian Aid, Catholic Action, Oxfam, War on Want, Spastics, Cancer Research, the Week's Good Cause.

Verse 9: The selfish and evil will envy the contentment and happiness of heart which such a life brings.

The believer reciting and meditating on psalms 111 and 112 will want to pray: 'Lord, make me such a person like this, make me like you, O holy, loving Lord'.

113   God's greatness and goodness

This psalm is a call to all God's servants to praise him. It may be a call to gentiles as well as to Israel, for he is to be praised all day and from now on for ever (vv.1–3).

The next three verses speak of God's greatness; there is none like him in earth or heaven. His dwelling place is high above the universe, yet he looks down in concern for men (vv.4—6).

God cares for the lowly, raising the poor and needy and setting them with princes, as in Hannah's song (1 Sam. 2.7—8) and lifts the poor from the dungheap, an echo perhaps from Job. There is a more direct reference to Hannah's longing for a child in verse 12, and perhaps a fatherly note in the psalmist's mention of a mother's joy in her family.

The Christian's thought goes naturally to the New Testament parallel of Hannah's song in the Magnificat, the Song of Mary of Nazareth rejoicing in the conception of the babe promised in her spiritual experience which Christians speak of as the Annunciation.

In our modern day, we can be aware of the many childless couples who long for a child and seek the aid of medical science in helping them to get one. So the psalmist concludes with Hallel, and we join him.

114   Memory of the Exodus

This psalm is a poem of great beauty recalling the most wonderful event in the whole of Israel's history — their liberation from slavery, and God's choice of them to be his own people in the sanctuary of Jerusalem. It may have been composed long after the event commemorated, when the exiles came back home in a second exodus, equally joyful.

The sea is personalized and is pictured as fleeing before the God of the advancing people and, at the end, the flow of Jordan is slowed down to allow them to cross safely into their new homeland.

Mountains are imagined as skipping like rams, and the little hills gambolling as young lambs in spring.

So the whole earth is bidden to tremble in awareness of God's presence in it, evidenced in the finding of springs of water gushing from the rock, nature thus obeying God's will and Israel blest in his activity.

As so often, poetry brings out the meaning and significance of some event or experience in a few rapturous verses more than a lengthy pedestrian description in prose – a *nota bene* to the commentator to cease his comments, and read the poet's rhapsody again!

115   Trust in emergency

This psalm is an exhortation to the congregation in the Temple, and to Israel generally, to put their trust in God in some emergency which is not specified. It is based on the belief that God is eternally faithful, loving and kind. Evidently, neighbouring nations seeing Israel's difficulties scoff at God's apparent inactivity, and jeer 'where is their God?', to which the psalmist replies 'Our God is in heaven. He does whatever he wills' (vv.1–2).

Verses 3–7 speak of the powerlessness of idols. They may be made of silver and gold, but they are the work of men; they cannot see or speak, they cannot hear men's prayers, they cannot touch, nor move to men's rescue. Those who make them and worship them will in time become like them, lifeless and ineffective.

So the writer calls to Israel, to the Temple priests and to all Godfearers to trust in God, their shield and help. He will bless them all and their children after them. The word 'bless' occurs five times in four verses (8–14).

God is the creator of heaven and earth; from heaven he directs and blesses his creatures, unlike the inert and ineffective idols. He has given the earth to men as the sphere in which they should express their worship and obedience. It is in this life that they are to do this, before life comes to an end and they go down into the silence of the grave. The last verse must therefore imply for himself and his fellow-worshippers in the Temple a resolution to bless God while they are still living (vv.15–17).

For the individual Christian and for choirs and congregations singing the psalms in church, the words 'for evermore' mean something very different, as they indeed do for Jewish worshippers today. Yet the Christian will welcome the emphasis of our Jewish friends on the duty of serving God faithfully while we have physical life. If we do not do so, there is little hope of blessedness.

It has been suggested that this psalm was sung antiphonally in the Temple, the choir singing verses 1–7 and 15–17, with the precentor and choir singing alternatively verses 8–14. Anglican solo voice, choir and congregation would need careful training to do this effectively!

116   Personal thanksgiving

Some writers have thought that the writer was Hezekiah giving thanks after his serious illness (2 Kings 20.1–11) but the Hebrew is said to show Aramaic characteristics, which would indicate a date after the exile. Whatever the case, the psalmist's experience proves that God does hear prayer, so he resolves to turn to God whenever he needs help (vv.1–2).

Verses 3–6 tell of his plight, near to death and how he kept calling to God for help.

Verses 7–10 speak of his confidence in peaceful trust. He was brought very low, and now he will be able to walk safely again in the land of the living. The second half of verse 10 suggests that his plight is due to evil men for in the heat of it, he was tempted to regard all men as deceitful and unreliable.

Verses 11–13 suggest that he would make vows if God would rescue him from his plight. The cup of salvation mentioned in verse 12 refers to the drink offering which he will bring to the Temple in gratitude for his release from the danger of death. Christians meditating on this psalm or reciting it in the offices of the Church connect this verse with the Eucharistic cup.

Verse 13, repeated in verse 17 speaks of the psalmist's resolve to return thanks to God openly before the whole congregation.

Verses 14–18 repeat his intention to offer a thanksgiving sacrifice in the Temple.

No notes or comments can exhaust the psalmist's spirit of thankfulness.

In verse 14 he pictures God's grief in the suffering and death of his faithful ones. The New Testament takes this further in its faith that God will see them safely through death, a thought already anticipated in Wisdom 3.1–2.

117 Praise

This shortest of all the psalms is also one of the greatest, a joyful Hallelujah in two verses, praising God for his mercy and truth which are eternal. It is a call to all nations to praise him, and is a witness to Israel's mission to the world and to its faith that God's loving kindness and faithfulness are available for all people, through all time.

118 Re-dedication festival

This psalm is a song of thanksgiving for some great national event. It may have been the celebration of the festival of Tabernacles described in Neh. 8.14–18, the restoration of worship under Nehemiah the governor and Ezra the priest in 44 BC, after the reading of the Book of the Law. Verses 23–24 describe it as a very great day, brought about by a marvellous act of God.

The same three classes of people summoned in psalm 115.8–10 are called upon again to give thanks, namely Israel, the house of Aaron and all who fear God (v.1–4).

Verses 5–18 have a personal note about them, but the psalmist may be speaking as representative of the whole nation, expressing his personal joy in the joint thanksgiving. He speaks of being in great danger, in which he experienced God as helper, convincing him that it is better to trust in God than in men or rulers. All nations surrounded him, like a swarm of bees, he was almost overcome, but the Lord delivered him, and he knows now that he will not die but live.

Verse 14 recalls the song of triumph sung by Moses and the people after the successful crossing of the Red Sea (Exod. 15.2). The new deliverance may have been hymned by a similar leader expressing the jubilation of all on a similar occasion.

Verses 19–25 suggest a great procession entering the gates of the Temple, singing in grateful thanksgiving, while verses 26–29 may refer to the service before the altar, culminating in personal terms again, 'You are my God and I will praise you: you are my God I will exalt you', a personal as well as a general re-dedication.

The first part of verse 26 'Blessed is he who comes in the name of the Lord' has a messianic reference. Luke in his gospel tells us, 'As he was now drawing near, at the descent of the Mount of Olives, the whole multitude of the disciples began to rejoice and praise God with a loud voice for all the mighty works they had seen, saying "Blessed is the king who comes in the name of the Lord"' (19.37–40). As we take part in the Eucharist, at the 'Holy, Holy, Holy', we thank God, using the same words of Christ, for all the benefits that he has brought and will continue to bring.

Verse 24 can sound a personal note of devotion again. 'This is a (the) day that the Lord has made, let us rejoice and be glad in it.' The loving, trusting disciple can say this of every day.

119 In praise of God's law

This is a verbal fugue in praise of the Torah, the Law of the Lord, consisting of twenty-two stanzas corresponding with the number of letters in the Hebrew alphabet, each stanza having eight verses all beginning with the same letter until the alphabet is completed.

In every verse there is a word that is a facet of God's law:

the way, guidelines for daily conduct, set out for man in the divine revelation
the Law, the whole will of God as imparted to man for his guidance and direction
the testimonies, the rules of conduct which attest the divine will
precepts, rules which it is man's duty to obey
statutes, 'that which is engraven', laws regulating the life of each individual
commandments, a general term for the laws of God in the religious life
ordinances, judgements which regulate man's relationship with his neighbour, characterized by righteousness
Word, the expressed will of God
judgements, the principles on which God governs the world.

139

The twenty-two stanzas may be summarized in the following titles and key verses:

1–8:   The blessedness of those who keep the Torah. Vv.1, 3: Those who seek God with their whole heart, and walk in his ways are blessed and happy.

9–16: How the psalmist values God. V.11: Do I treasure God's words in my heart, and find more joy in them than in my money?

17–35: The Torah is a joyful burden. V.18: A prayer that the cataract in my spiritual eyes may be removed, so that I can see the wonders of God's love.

25–32: Life in God's Law. V.32: When the Lord liberates my heart I shall want to walk in his ways and be enabled to do so.

33–40: Life in God's Law. V.36: A prayer to incline my heart to keep God's commands rather than to selfish greed.

41–48: The results of obedience. V.43: A prayer that I may always speak God's truth and set my hope on his guidance.

49–56: The Torah brings comfort and hope. V.55: The psalmist thinks of God whenever he wakes in the night, and sets his mind to keep God's laws in the day.

57–64: The psalmist's response to God. V.59: The writer examines his way of life and turns again to God.

65–72: The goodness of God. Vv.67 and 72: The psalmist has been in trouble, and the very troubles have taught him how to live a godly life.

73–80: 'I am Your Creation.' V.80: If my heart is sound in God's laws, I shall never be put to shame, and never let God down.

81–88: The psalmist's suffering. V.83: I am like a wine-skin hung up in the smoky roof, shrunken and dry, yet if I remember God's law I shall be made useful again.

89–96: God's faithfulness. V.96: The divine perfection exceeds and outlasts all human perfections.

97–104: God instructs the soul. V.100: When God is my teacher, I become wiser than all human teachers and the most revered of my seniors in age and experience.

105–112: Light and joy at every step. V.105: As a torch on a dark night helps me to walk safely, so is God's word within my heart.

113–120: No dealings with evil doers. V.117: If God holds me up I shall be safe wherever I go, and whatever happens to me.

121–128: It is time for God to act. V.126: With so many violations of God's Law, the psalmist prays God to act quickly.

129–136: The psalmist is longing for God's Law. V.135: The brightness of God's face dispels darkness, ignorance and depression, and the psalmist prays to be taught God's laws.

137–144: God's righteous judgements. V.141: The writer recognizes that he is a man of little importance, but protests that he always remembers God's teaching.

145–152: Waiting for God. Vv.147–148: Before darkness falls and before morning light dawns, the poet has made a habit of prayer.

153–160: 'Come to my rescue!' Three times in this short section the psalmist prays that God will give him life and quicken his whole being into willing obedience and eager activity.

161–168: The joy of God's Word. V.162: When the writer sees the meaning and relevance of

God's words in the heart, he is as glad as someone who has accidentally come across a great treasure.

169–176: 'Go on seeking me.' V.176: Looking back on his life he sees that he has often strayed and become lost like a foolish sheep. He fears that he may do so again in the future and prays that God will seek him as he has done in the past.

The psalmist clearly knew psalm 19.7–10, which speaks of God's Law as more desirable than much fine gold and sweeter than honey. Jewish commentators think he lived in the 5th century BC and was probably a scribe in Ezra's school.

The psalm contains many gems of devotion, among which the following are typical of the writer's spirituality:

V.24: For your commandments are my delight:
and they are counsellors in my defence.

V.32: Let me run the way of your commandments:
for you will liberate my heart.

V.72: The law of your mouth is dearer unto me:
than a wealth of gold and silver.

V.94: I am yours O save me: for I have sought
your precepts.

V.105: Your word is a lantern to my feet:
and a light to my path.

V.135: Make your face shine upon your servant:
and teach me your statutes.

V.147: Before the morning light I rise and I call:
for in your word is my hope.

V.162: I am as glad of your word:
as one who finds rich spoil. (cf. Matt. 13.44)

V.176: I have gone astray like a sheep that is lost:
O seek your servant. (cf. Luke 15.3–7)

A Jewish commentator makes a very telling observation on the whole psalm: 'The psalmist loves God's Law because he loves God'.

Monastic practice based on verse 164 has been for seven regular times of prayer each day, during which the whole of this psalm has been recited, a custom not so fully observed in the present as in the past.

In the New Testament, Jesus devotes a large number of parables to illustrate the meaning of the Kingdom of God, the rule of God in the hearts and affairs of men, a clear continuation of the Old Testament concept of the Law of the Lord.

120   Song of ascent

The fifteen psalms, 120–134, form a group which were sung as the pilgrims drew near to the holy city at the three great festivals of the year, Passover, Weeks and Tabernacles (Exod. 23.17, Deut. 16.16–17). They may collectively be called 'Songs of Ascent'. The writer of psalm 120 says that he has had to live among cruel and barbarous neighbours, such as those living as far away as the Black Sea or among Arabian tribes (Mesheck and Kedar). He himself is a man of peace, who has had to live too long among unfriendly people. The implication is that he is relieved and glad to be away from these hostile surroundings and to enjoy for a while the more peaceful conditions of Jerusalem.

121   Israel's guardian

This psalm is an expression of trust in God on the part of people who feel the need of more than human help.

The writer is in trouble and asks the question 'Where shall I find help?' The answer is that the needed help will come from God the Creator (vv.1–2).

God who is in charge of Israel never sleeps. He will always be ready to come to its defence. He will be like shade from the hot sun by day and will guard against the effects of the moon, associated in the popular mind with lunacy. All one's undertakings, going out from home to work in the morning, and returning in the evening to the family life and duties, will be under God's protecting care. He will guard our life from the moment of setting out on a journey until its completion.

Countless souls all down the ages have gained comfort from this psalm, and so have looked to the future with assurance of God's love.

122   Joy on arrival

The author recalls with joy the invitation to join with others in a pilgrimage to Jerusalem. Even if the journey were from Galilee it would not be free from danger, and if it were from a neighbouring country, the security of travelling together and being able to talk to congenial companions on the last tiring stretch of each day would be very welcome.

Now at last their feet are standing within the city walls, their eyes searching for the first glimpse of the Temple, for Jerusalem is a compact city, barely a mile square in area. So the psalmist reflects on what it means to him and those with him. All the bodies of pilgrims have one aim – to worship in the Temple with all its associations. It is also a centre of unity for the scattered tribes. It is there that rulers and judges have made wise and just judgments in the past, and decided between the claims and complaints of aggrieved citizens (vv.2–5).

At this point, the leader or the poet, expressing the joy of the party, calls to them to halt for a moment to pray for Jerusalem. His bidding is 'Peace be within your walls; may all your people prosper!' 'Shalom!', however, means more than just peaceful conditions. It includes a sense of happiness, blessing and well-being, all that the heart may rightly desire.

So he addresses the city on behalf of his companions, and vows to work for its welfare, for it is the house of God, where the divine presence and blessing are experienced (vv.6–9).

Pilgrims still go to Jerusalem in hundreds of thousands every year. They too will reflect on its long history of troubles, prophets and priests, and long for it to be true to its name 'City of Peace' in Hebrew, and 'El Quds', 'the Holy', in Arabic. When they are there and after their visit, they will feel moved to pray for its peace, believing that if a just peace can come there, it will be a gospel message to all the troubled places of the world. Christians will remember our Lord's love of Jerusalem and his tears over it and the world.

All may remember John's vision of the holy city, with its twelve gates never shut, and all the nations streaming into it, with the river of peace and grace flowing through its centre, with trees flourishing on its banks, whose leaves are for the healing of the nations. They may remember also another writer's description of the heavenly Jerusalem, the mother of us all, the final home of the human spirit, the homeland that all of us are seeking.

123   Looking up to God

The writer of this psalm and his fellow countrymen are in great trouble; not only are they oppressed but they are regarded with contempt by their oppressors (vv.3–5). The historical occasion of their plight is not explained. It may have been the opposition of the Samaritans when they returned from exile and were making strenuous efforts to rebuild the city walls and restore the Temple (Neh. 2.10).

So the psalmist, like the writer of psalm 121, lifts up his eyes, in this case directly to God, enthroned in the heavens. He likens himself and his companions to servants, looking to the hand of their masters and mistresses, dependent on them to protect them and supply all their needs. So he prays for God's mercy on them, pleading that they cannot endure much longer their cruel treatment and the contempt heaped upon them (vv.1–3).

So the human soul in its distress and humiliation looks up to God for mercy and relief, in dependence and trust.

124   A great danger past

Again the danger in this psalm is not specified. The psalmist, however, feels that it was one which might well have overwhelmed the nation. He likens it to a torrent coming down from the hills after heavy rain, resulting in loss of life and damage to property (vv.1–3).

Verses 4–6 are a thanksgiving to God for a wonderful escape, which the psalmist compares to the escape of a bird from the snare set by a game-keeper or poacher.

He concludes with a verse which has become a versicle and response in Christian worship: 'Our help is in the name of the Lord, who has made heaven and earth'. This verse is used in the Anglican service of Confirmation, looking forward to God's protecting care for the young and old, who are affirming their loyalty to him.

146

An aerial photograph of Jerusalem taken from a distance shows Mount Zion, on which the city stands, as surrounded by many peaks as if they were guarding it. To the psalmist, the thus encircled mount is a symbol of permanence which cannot be shaken. In the same way, he says, the Lord encircles his people with divine protection (vv.1–2).

It looks as if some threat of foreign domination, accompanied by injustice, was weakening the faith of some people. The psalmist assures them that 'the sceptre of wickedness', the symbol of that domination, shall have no power over them. He prays that God will defend all who are good and upright in heart, and preserve their independence (vv.3–4).

He goes on to pray that those who turn away from God in evil ways may incur divine condemnation, and ends his prayer by invoking God's peace upon faithful Israel, a peace of freedom, security and blessedness. His firm conviction is that in time of trouble the surest source of security and blessing is God.

126 Past joy, present sorrow, joy once more

This writer bids the nation look back to the great time when God delivered them from captivity in exile, and brought them back to their own land. It was such a great moment that they could hardly believe it to be real, they thought they must have been dreaming. When convinced of the reality of it, they laughed with joy and burst into songs of praise. The surrounding nations were impressed, admitting that God had done a great thing for Israel, and that made them rejoice all the more (vv.1–4).

Now they are in trouble once more, and pray that their fortunes may be restored yet again. The psalmist bids them remember the streams in the Negev, the southern part of the country, which in the winter fill the wadis, but which become dried up in the hot summer. The rains come again, and the life-giving water can be irrigated into the dusty fields.

The peasant may have to wait in hope and then set to work when the rain comes, with hard labour and tiredness of body. He is tired out with ploughing and sowing, but his efforts will produce a harvest. Proverbially speaking, he may have to sow in tears, but he will reap with joy.

So it will be in national affairs, if the nation is patient, enduring and trusting in God. While the pilgrim is in Jerusalem, faith and hope can be reborn.

127   Futile without God

Most scholars think that this short psalm consists of two shorter psalms, with different themes. The first (vv.1–3) deals with the rebuilding after a period of destruction; the second with the birth of children as a gift of God (vv.3–5). Both, however, may be descriptive of the period of reconstruction under Nehemiah, when there was a great need of houses, and also of a large enough population to defend the city and carry on its work.

It is interesting to be told that there is no definite article in Hebrew, and that the psalmist is speaking of 'a' house as any house, and of 'a' city as any city. His point is that unless God's protection and blessing are available, the builders, however hard they work, labour in vain. It is the same with a city: however faithfully the watchmen do their duty, without God's protecting aid, their task is without success (vv.1–3).

148

The BCP has a phrase which one regrets losing – 'for so He giveth his beloved sleep', which may mean nothing more than the rest that comes in sleep, but some scholars interpret it as meaning 'while they sleep' or 'during sleep'. This suggests that the Spirit of God continues his inspiring, revealing, problem-solving activity even while we sleep. Many would tell us that they had retired to sleep with some problem or concern on their minds, and wakened in the morning with new light and guidance.

The second short part of this short psalm deals with the blessing of children. They are said to be like arrows in the quiver of a warrior, indicating that they are able to safeguard him in old age and to stand by his side in disputes which have to be referred to judges who preside at the gate of the city to decide in such cases. God is seen to be involved in the birth of children; indeed the Rabbis held that every child had three parents, God in addition to father and mother.

So the psalmist teaches that man's labour without the help and blessing of God is lost. It behoves all who believe in him to seek his wisdom and help, and to be thankful for his providence in family life.

128 Happy families

The theme of this short psalm is that the man who reverences God and decides to live in accordance with God's will and Law, will be blessed in home and family life. A large family is regarded by the writer and his contemporaries as a great blessing, and the wife is likened to a vine with many clusters of lovely grapes, and children sitting round the table are compared with fresh green olive plants. This ideal picture takes monogamy for granted.

With such blessing from God, the writer believes that Jerusalem will be a happy and prosperous city. With such a family, the writer promises a happy old age, with parents secure and happy in the support of grandchildren.

He also sees that the welfare of the city and nation are bound up with a happy and godly family life. In our present age, we are seeing the relevance of this happy little psalm. There are problems of relationship between parents and children, and of social provision for family life. All need to be worked out and governed by faith in God, from whom all parenthood derives.

Happy and godly families make a happy and righteous nation. Those with happy families will thank God for them, and others pray for God's wisdom and grace to make them so.

129   Freed by God

The psalmist is looking back on Israel's sufferings, especially those in the early years of the nation when they were slaves in Egypt. He pictures their backs cut by the lashes from their taskmasters, just as the earth is furrowed by the plough. In a second figure of speech, he talks of cords, the ropes which harness the ox to the plough. 'But', he adds, 'they have not prevailed' . . . 'the righteous God has cut us free.'

Verses 5–8 are the writer's imprecations on Israel's enemies. May they fail in their plots against Israel! May they wither like seeds blown on to the flat roofs, falling into cracks and crevices, and burnt up by the hot sun. So may Israel's foes perish, be short-lived as the roof-top grass! May the seeds of corn shrivel and produce no harvest!

In the Middle East, passers-by usually call out a

blessing on the workers, as Boaz greeted the reapers in his fields at Bethlehem: 'The Lord be with you!' to which they would answer 'The Lord bless you!' (Ruth 2.4). Let there be no such friendly greeting and blessing expressed to Israel's enemies! (v.6). Vengeance on enemies is the wish and prayer.

In spite of these imprecations, the message of the psalm is one of hope and trust that the God who has come to Israel's protection so often in the past will continue to do so in the present and future.

130 Out of the depths

This psalm is a heartfelt expression of penitence for sin, and a prayer for forgiveness from an individual. Not only is he conscious of his own sins and troubles but those of the nation as well.

The first two verses are his cry of distress and an appeal to God to hear him. He is out of his depth, overwhelmed with troubles, about to sink under the stormy waves that beat upon him. Like the writer of another psalm, he feels that 'all your waves and breakers have gone over me' (42.9). Like Nehemiah too (1.6), he prays, 'let thy ears be attentive to hear the prayer of thy servant'.

In verses 3—4 he realizes that if God were to mark all our sins, none of us could stand such a test. But he has faith that God is a forgiving God, and his fear of God's judgment becomes reverence, a holy fear. God forgives that men may be led to reverence him.

So, as he tells us in verses 5—6, he waits for the Lord, he hopes to hear God's forgiving word. He longs for God's promise as eagerly as watchmen on the city walls look for the first rays of the sun, when they can be relieved of their sentinel duty.

In the last two verses he appeals to his fellow-religionists to share his experience, for with God there is mercy and unlimited readiness to forgive. He is conscious of the nation's sins and failures as much as his own.

In personal devotion, the first verse of this penitential psalm may suggest the depth of the heart, the very core of being, where our communion with God takes place, where the Spirit of God indwells us in his saving love, inspiring us to holiness and deep happiness.

131 God's motherly comfort

This little psalm has been described as 'a gem of exquisite beauty and surpassing loveliness'. The psalmist pictures a child, no longer fed from its mother's breast, but from time to time held close in her arms, perhaps sucking its little thumb, as children who have been weaned often do. So the child of God is calmed and quieted in the thought of God's comforting love. He/she is conscious of a quiet and peaceful heart.

The writer is a humble man. He does not look for high office in the community, nor desire any prominence. In saying this, he may be admitting to himself that ambitious hopes had entered his mind in the past, but now he has weaned it from such desires, so he enjoys an inner serenity.

Some commentators make the point that this psalm is hardly a prayer. Yet it opens with the word 'Lord', so the psalmist is conscious of God's presence and what follows is a quiet reflection of grateful trust.

He ends with an appeal to his own people to follow his example and wait continually on God to bless and guide them for the future.

The psalmist remembers all the hardships endured by King David in the capture of Jerusalem, and in his persistent plan to build a worthy house for God, and a shrine for the Ark which he had recaptured from the Philistines. Many a sleepless night had he spent considering how this should be done (vv.1–4).

Verses 5–6 are perhaps a response by the pilgrims as they remember the discovery of the Ark at Ephrathah (Bethlehem), and its being brought back to a sanctuary in Jerusalem, until the Temple was built. Now they are ready to worship God there, inspired by the memory of David.

Verses 7–9 are said to be prayers on arrival in the Temple, with a prayer for priests and worshippers: 'Let your priests be clothed with righteousness, and let your faithful ones shout for joy', a versicle and response still included in Morning and Evening Prayer. This is followed by a prayer for the reigning king.

The verses 10–19 the psalmist and people remember God's promise to David: 'If your children will keep my covenant and the commands which I will teach them, their children also shall sit upon your throne for ever'. This is a very stiff condition and no one reading later history could claim that it had been faithfully fulfilled.

The divine promise goes on to declare that the presence of God in Zion will bring material blessings upon the people. The prayer in verse 8 is answered in verse 16. In addition, a lamp is promised, which symbolizes both the continuing presence of God and the preservation of David's dynasty.

Anyone who has lived in modern Israel, even for a short time will be familiar with the claim that the return to the homeland and the restoration of the nation were brought about by God's will and blessing. The warning in verse 13 and the promise of a lamp to give light to the problems of the present and the future, need to be equally emphasized. So we today, pray for the peace of Jerusalem and the acceptance of the vocation of Abraham and his descendants to be a blessing to all other nations.

133 Living in unity

For the three great festivals, Jews came together from many different countries and from every part of Israel. For the days of each festival they would be living together in Jerusalem and worshipping in the Temple. Members of any family might be re-united after years of separation. The poet speaks of the beauty of this unity. He likens it to the consecrating oil poured upon the head of the High Priest, reaching into his beard and down the whole length of his sacred vestments, symbolizing the effects of this living harmoniously together on the whole nation (vv.1–2).

He goes on to compare this re-union to the abundant dew of Mount Hermon, which not only benefits the soil and vegetation on it, but falls on distant hills. Hermon was two hundred miles from Jerusalem, and the poet cannot mean that its dew reached as far as that, but that the living together in Zion had a similar benefit on the whole nation and beyond. The blessing of God will radiate from his Temple for evermore. The writers of the psalms are said to have had no clear belief in an after life; one wonders, however, if the phrase 'life for evermore' was beginning to suggest a seed of eternity which would ultimately flower into full belief, as it did among devout Pharisees and in the teaching of Jesus.

134 Blessing for the journey home

This is the last of the Songs of Ascent. We may perhaps picture a final act of worship in the Temple on the last day of the festival, which went on beyond sunset, as if the pilgrims were reluctant to go away. The priests and Levites would continue their duties throughout the night, and the departing pilgrims would give a final salutation and charge to them: 'Lift up your hands towards the Holy of Holies and bless the Lord', to which the ministers would respond 'May the Lord, the Creator of Heaven and earth, bless you (always) from Zion'. So, conscious of the divine blessing, the pilgrims would leave the Temple courts, ready for a night's sleep before they set out on the long journey home.

135 Summons to praise God

This psalm traces the hand of God in nature and in Israel's history. It opens with a call to praise God, addressing priests and Levites in the first place, on the ground that God is gracious and good, and has chosen Israel as his own special possession (vv.1–4).

God's power is seen in nature, in earth and sky and sea. He is above all the powers of nature which some people think of as gods. He sends rain, wind and lightning out of his treasures (vv.5–7).

God has been active in Israel's history, especially in their liberation from Egypt, in their defeat of nations and their kings who opposed them, finally settling them in Canaan (vv.8–12).

He then contrasts God's eternity with the impotence of idols, using the same words as in psalm 115.4–8 (vv.13–18).

Finally, he calls on Israel, with the priests, Levites and all who fear God to bless the Lord who has made Jerusalem his dwelling place, the centre of his worship, from which his power extends over all (vv.19—21). This psalm is set for the closing worship for the sabbath in synagogues today.

136   The great hallel-lu-jah

Each of the 26 verses of this psalm has the refrain 'for his mercy endures for ever'. We can imagine the cantor (a very important minister in the Temple, in the synagogues when the Temple was destroyed, and in the synagogues today) intoning God's great acts one after another, and then the choir of priests, Levites and singers joining in the loud refrain.

The first three verses are a call to thanksgiving to the God of gods, the Lord of lords, who is eternally good.

Then follow sections praising him as Creator (vv.4—9), delivering Israel from Egypt (vv.10—15), leading them victoriously through the desert (vv.16—22), supporting them in times of humiliation, rescuing them from enemies, providing food 'to all that lives'. He is God of heaven, and thus passes from national sovereignty to universal Lordship, inviting all that live to join in the Great Hallel (vv.23—26).

137   Bitter memories

A Jewish commentator says that to understand this psalm we need to think of an exile returned from Babylon, seeing the ruins of the city which he loves and to which he had longed to return, and remembering the cruel tortures inflicted on the exiles by their captors.

The prophet Jeremiah spoke of Babylon as a city 'that dwellest upon many waters', a reference to the many streams and canals which irrigated the countryside around (51.13).

The returned exile described how he and his companions sat mourning on the ground as they remembered the dreadful calamities which had fallen on the beloved city of Jerusalem. They had played mournful dirges on their harps, but when asked to sing more lively songs to amuse their captors, they had refused, hanging their instruments on the poplar trees around. How could they be expected to sing the songs they used to sing in the Temple, in a foreign land, merely to amuse their captors? (vv.1–4).

Their love of Jerusalem is then movingly expressed in verses 5–6. Sooner than forget the holy city, the psalmist says, he would rather lose the use of his right hand and all power to speak or sing. For Jerusalem is his chiefest joy.

The last three verses of the psalm are some of the most vindictive in the whole Psalter. Like the prophet Obadiah, he calls down the vengeance of God on the people of Edom, who abetted the Babylonians in the destruction of Jerusalem when they ought to have come to the defence of their brother Israel.

The psalmist's most scathing denunciation, however, is for the Babylonians themselves. He hopes to see them suffer in the same way as they have inflicted cruel barbarities on Israel, which included hurling infant children against the rocks.

Shocked as the reader of this psalm may be at these vindictive curses, if we try to imagine ourselves in the writer's place and feel his horror at the cruelties he witnessed, we may find some excuse for his bitterness.

138 Thanksgiving, trust, hope

This is a lovely psalm which arouses not the slightest misgiving or criticism in the mind of the believing and worshipping soul who recites it and meditates upon it today, until its very last line shows the writer struggling against the commonly accepted views of many in his time, that God on occasion forsakes his people.

It falls into three parts: verses 1–3 give wholehearted thanksgiving to God; verses 4–6 indicate the writer's hope and expectation that kings and rulers will come to acknowledge God's greatness and glory; verses 7–8 show his trust that God will protect him in danger and fulfil his purpose for him.

He was obviously in the habit of turning towards Jerusalem when he prayed, as many Jews still do, and as Muslims look towards Mecca. He is thankful for past times when God answered his prayers 'and put new strength into my soul', reminiscent of Isa. 40.31, 'They that wait upon the Lord shall renew their strength'.

In the second section, he expresses his faith that when rulers hear, study and obey the words of the Lord, they will acknowledge one greater than themselves and praise him. Verse 6 adds his faith that God, exalted above all, cares for the lowly, and opposes those who are proud of their own greatness, a conviction echoed in the Christian psalm that we call the Magnificat.

Verse 7 shows his faith that however great the danger he is in, and however furious the forces that threaten him, God will be there with his protecting hand. Finally, he sees a divine purpose in his life and prays that God will complete it. The last line is really saying to God, 'You will not forsake those you are creating'. The individual meditating on this lovely psalm will be moved to pray, 'God give me such a faith as this'.

139   The all-knowing omnipresent God

This psalm has been described as the noblest utterance in the Psalter of pure contemplative theism, animated but not daunted by the thought of God's omnipresence and omniscience. It strikes many readers as coming from an intimate relationship with God, rather than a reasoned meditation. Most scholars consider that its date is after the exile. It divides into five quite clear sections:

Verses 1–6: God's omniscience: all the psalmist's thoughts, words, goings and doings are known to him.

Verses 7–11: His omnipresence, like the sun which covers the whole sky in the course of a day. Man cannot hide from God, even if he tries to do so. Darkness and light are alike to him. He sees all. Yet with all the self-accusation, there is assurance of God's leading and protecting.

Verses 12–18: God knows each one of us from the moment of conception, while the embryo is being formed in the hiddenness of the mother's womb. God's thoughts cannot be weighed or numbered.

Verses 19–22: The psalmist hates the wicked and prays to God to slay them. A more acceptable attitude is seen in 21b, which the BCP translates as 'And am not I grieved with those that rise up against Thee?' The ASB suggests a greater loathing, in which the writer counts God's enemies as his own.

Verses 23–24: He prays for God's scrutiny of himself, so that any lurking wickedness may be recognized and overcome.

These last two verses may remind the reader of the collect with which every Eucharist opens, one which goes back to Pope Gregory who sent Augustine to convert us English;

159

Almighty God . . . unto whom all hearts are open, all
desires known, . . . and from whom no secrets are
hid; . . . cleanse the thoughts of our hearts . . . by the
inspiration of thy Holy Spirit, . . . that we may perfectly love Thee . . . and worthily magnify thy holy
Name.

The Christian reader would probably want to add a
verse that comes from a hymn going back to the patron
saint of Ireland:

> Christ be with me, Christ within me,
>   Christ behind me, Christ before me,
> Christ beside me, Christ to win me,
>   Christ to comfort and restore me,
> Christ beneath me, Christ above me,
>   Christ in quiet, Christ in danger,
> Christ in hearts of all that love me,
>   Christ in mouth of friend and stranger.

In short, Christ omnipresent with God, and with the
omniscience of God.

140   Prayer for protection

This psalm and the following three seem to be a group
reflecting similar conditions: they are attributed to
David; all four deal with the subject of the persecution
of pious people at the hands of the ungodly; they have
similarities in style and language. It has been suggested
that the same psalmist wrote all four. He may have seen
in the sufferings of David some relevance to his own
troubles very much later.

In verses 1—5 the writer describes the plots of the

wicked and appeals to God for help, saying that God is his God who will hear his prayer, for he is a sure stronghold, a protector in times of attack, who will not let the poisonous words and insidious plots of the wicked succeed.

Then he prays against his enemies: may the mischief they plot for others fall on them, may they be cast into a miry pit and be unable to clamber out, may burning coals descend on them, let them never recover from these well-deserved punishments. Verse 11 shows his desire for a land free from violence and evil.

Having thus relieved his feelings at the injustices he is suffering under, the psalmist, in a calmer mind, expresses his confidence in God, whose will is to relieve the oppressed and to make sure that the poor get their rights, for then the righteous will live in God's sight, blessed and peaceful, praising him with grateful hearts.

141 A better prayer

If the four psalms we are considering are from the same author, we may detect a difference in tone in this second one. In the first four verses, his prayer for help is as urgent as before, but now he prays that God will set a guard on his speech and keep him from getting involved with wrongdoers. It looks as if he was often present at the offering of the evening sacrifice in the Temple, but is now unable to be present, so he prays that his prayer may be as pleasing to God. He may even be praying that he may not be tempted to retaliate.

In verses 5–7 he says before God that he is willing to accept reproof and advice from righteous people, if there is anything unworthy in his conduct. Such reproof is like finest oil on his head, compared with what evil men

161

want to heap upon him. God the Mighty One will judge the wicked, and then they will regret they did not take notice of what the psalmist had warned them of. It is difficult to understand verse 8: Rabbi Cohen interprets it 'as chips of wood are scattered all around when logs are cut up, so the bones of his murdered friends lie in abundance at the entrance of Sheol', into which the evildoers are doomed to fall.

Verses 9–11 tell of the psalmist's look to God, whom he prays not to drain away his life but to keep him safe from the snares and traps set for him.

142   Still in desperate straits

The psalmist is not yet out of his trouble, in fact it seems worse than ever. Plots against him continue, there seems to be no way of escape. No one is near to sympathize and care for him. His courage is low, he feels shut up in prison, like the prophet Jeremiah (vv.3–5, 7–8).

In all this, he still goes on praying to God: 'I pour out my complaint before him, and tell him all my trouble,' a very wise practice for those of us who find ourselves in similar situations (v.2). He cries more loudly and prays more urgently for defence and aid.

The last verse shows that he believes that God will help and reward him, one result of which will be that the righteous will gather round him and rejoice with him in all that God has done.

143   Further prayers

Relief has not yet come. The psalmist still feels in darkness, his heart is appalled by what is happening, enemies still pursue him, his spirit grows faint (vv.1, 3-5). In all this mental anguish, he begins to see that he too needs forgiveness: 'Bring not your servant into judgment, for in your sight can no man living be justified' (v.2), a prayer often used in Anglican Morning and Evening Prayer, as a preparatory sentence before confession.

He remembers God's mercies in the past, but this only makes him realize his need of God in the present: 'I stretch out my hands towards you, my soul yearns for you like a thirsty land'. He longs to hear of God's mercies every morning, for in God is his trust and hope. So he prays another good prayer, that God will show him the way ahead. That good prayer leads to another 'Teach me to do your will, for you are my God, let your kindly spirit lead me in an even path', in which I shall not stumble. A third petition follows, namely that, true to the revelation of his name and character, God will bring him safely out of his troubles (vv.5-11).

One could wish that his prayer might have ended there, but he still can't help praying that God will slay his enemies. Yet his last words recover even from that revengeful prayer, for he adds, 'Truly I am your servant'.

144   Victory in God

This psalm is attributed to David, perhaps because of his victory over Goliath. David, however, is mentioned in the third person, and also victory to kings, which suggests that it may have been written in his spirit and style (v.10). It is a joyful psalm, largely a mosaic of quotations from other psalms.

The first two verses speak of God as the rock, strength, stronghold, fortress, deliverer, shield, refuge, who also gives help in time of war, and who has the ability to govern. Verses 3–4 speak of the insignificance of man, as insubstantial as a breath of wind, and as shortlived as a passing shadow (see also psalm 8.5).

So the psalmist prays for deliverance from alien enemies, much in the imagery of psalm 18.15, 17, who are characterized as being masters in perjury and falsehood (vv.5–8). Verses 9–12 speak of confidence in victory over present troubles, in a similar way to past victories granted to David and other kings.

The remaining verses (13–16) speak of the effect on Israel of God's protection, presenting the picture of a happy, prosperous nation with young men like sturdy saplings and young women as beautiful as carved figures on the pillars of palaces. The barns will be full of stored wheat and food, sheep will lamb in tens of thousands in the fields, cattle will calve abundantly, there will be no miscarriage (presumably in human birth), there will be no panic in the cities. Such will be the happy future of all who have the Lord for their God, echoing psalm 33.12.

145   A rosary of glorias

This psalm is the only one in the Psalter to be given the title 'A psalm of praise'. It is simply and splendidly that, verse after verse adding another reason for praising God, all the verses strung together like the beads on a rosary. It is an alphabetical poem, each verse beginning with another letter of the Hebrew alphabet. It is the first of the group of six psalms which conclude the Psalter, all of them praising, blessing and thanking God, in the same joyful spirit that makes many think that they were written by the same psalmist. It is a mosaic from other psalms, and sums up the message of the whole Psalter, which is entitled 'A Book of Praises'.

It is almost impossible to do it justice. It cannot be analysed into sections, for every verse stands in its own right. Every reader will pick out verses which ring bells in his own heart. For example, the opening verse addressing God as 'my King'; 'The Lord is loving to every man, and his mercy is over all his works (v.9); The Lord is just in all his ways' (v.17); 'The Lord is near to all who call upon Him' (v.18), and the final verse, 'My mouth shall speak the praises of the Lord, and let all flesh bless Him for his holy name for ever and ever'.

This glorious psalm is included three times in the Jewish liturgy for every day. A rabbi has said 'Whoever recites this psalm thrice daily may be assured that he is a son of the world to come'. Meditation on it daily will reveal new depths and relevance, and help to mould the character and sanctify the life of all who study it thoughtfully and thankfully.

146   God the never failing helper

The psalmist begins his song by urging himself to praise God as long as he lives, even when there is only a spark of life left in him (vv.1–2).

This thought about his own duration of life leads him on to realize that all are mortal, including those in power. There will come a day when mortals breathe their last, the vitality leaves their bodies, which turn to dust in coffins and graves. Then, in the commonly accepted beliefs of his time, all their thoughts and purposes come to an end (vv.3–4).

So he urges himself and others to put their whole trust and hope in God. This alone brings blessedness and happiness. He goes on to describe the utter reliability and goodness of God, who is not only the God of Israel, but the Creator of the universe and the lover of all its peoples, with special care for those in need of compassion and help – the hungry, captives, disabled, widows and orphans, those burdened with anxiety and fear, including strangers and foreigners. 'As for the wicked', he says, 'He turns their way upside down'. May there not be here the dawning of a belief that God's will is to turn wickedness into righteousness, and the hope that this will ultimately happen? (vv.5–11).

The last verse makes the psalm appropriate for corporate worship in the Temple. God's reign is eternal; he who has revealed himself in Zion is the God of all; ultimately all will accept his rule. Hallelujah, Praise to Him!

147 God's goodness, power and love

This psalmist advances four reasons to support his declaration that it is right and good to praise God:

1. His goodness in bringing back the exiles to Jerusalem and in blessing the work of reconstruction, as well as healing the sorrows of captivity. For this last point it is relevant to look at the promises of Isaiah (1.1–2).

2. His infinite wisdom and power in the ordering of the universe and in the powers of nature. As an example he mentions the innumerable stars, which no human being can count, whereas God knows their number and has given them their names. He also controls man's welfare, and directs the processes of nature which provide food for both men and animals. There is an interesting reference in verse 9 to 'the young ravens that call to him'. Evidently, ravens live in lonely and rocky places where food is scarce, and so they fly restlessly seeking food, with their plaintive cawing, which the psalmist

166

interprets as a prayer to God. He goes on to say that God's delight is not chiefly in the strength of a horse used in battle, in the strong limbs of a soldier (or an athlete) but on those who reverence him and wait upon him for wisdom and strength (vv.4–11).

3. God's goodness to Jerusalem, in strengthening the defences against attack, in making it possible for its people to live in peace, with plentiful supplies of food and his commands to the elements which produce the rich harvest. It looks as if this psalm was written during or soon after a hard winter, for he mentions ice, snow and hail, but also that 'at his word' these elements melt, the waters flow again and the wind brings warmer breezes (vv.12–18).

4. God's revelation to Israel and his commandments, obedience to which will result in righteous living. Israel has been favoured above all other nations, and the last verse implies a special responsibility on this account. Rabbi Cohen in his commentary quotes with approval the comment of a Christian scholar: 'The Psalmist is not rejoicing that other nations have not received these (ordinances), but that Israel has. Its privilege is its responsibility. It has received them that it may obey them, and then that it may make them known'.

The psalmist's last word is the same as his first — 'Hallelujah! Praise the Lord!'

148   Heaven and earth in harmony

If all copies of the *Benedicite* (The Song of the Three Children customarily sung in many churches during Lent and Advent) were lost, this psalm could well take its place. For in it all the planets in the sky, all the powers of nature, all the angels of heaven, all the rulers of the nations and their judges, all children, all people young and old, Israel with its special reasons for gratitude to God, all are called upon to join in a universal hymn of praise. Nothing in the BBC Songs of Praise on Sunday evenings could rival this glorious outburst of song.

Verses 1–6 are a call to the heavens to praise God their Creator, who has promulgated the constitution of each, which can never be abrogated.

Verses 7–11 speak of the praise which should come from the earth – the elements, the animal world, and all the inhabitants. There is a special mention of all sea monsters, which arouse human wonder, like the whale and the hippopotamus: all are called to praise God in the revelation of himself.

Verses 12–13 declare that God's glory is above the praises of heaven and earth. Israel has a special reason for joining in this praise of God, for he has given them a special place in his purposes, for God has proved that his presence has brought them near to himself in frequent rescues. So they are to be his obedient servants. Hallelujah! Praise the Lord!

149 A tremendous victory

A great victory has been won, to be celebrated by a new song of triumph in which the whole nation is called to take part. There will be dancing in the streets and in the Temple courts, accompanied by musicians with harps and drums. The psalmist ascribes the victory to God who is now seen to be showing favour to his people and honouring the humble and oppressed by his rescue. Now that the enemies have been defeated, people will be able to sleep safely in their beds (vv.1–5).

It is not easy to identify the occasion. Some scholars have thought that it was the victory of Nehemiah over the Samaritans who tried to obstruct the re-building of the city. It might have been the victory of Judas Maccabeus in the second century BC, described in the second book of the Maccabees: 'Judas and his men met the enemy in battle with invocation to God and prayers. So fighting with their hands and praying to God in their hearts, they laid low no less than 35,000 men, and were greatly gladdened by God's manifestation'. The psalmist speaks of high praises to God in their mouths, and an all devouring sword in their hands.

So the psalmist feels that the victory is not yet complete. Israel must remain armed and wipe out the remaining troops. In his mind, as in the case of the later Isaiah, he believes that God's vengeance must be carried out (vv.6–7, Isa. 61.2b, 63.4) until their leaders are paraded in chains in a triumphal march through the city and until the judgement decreed by God is carried out.

The reader today can indeed rejoice in the victory over powerful and cruel enemies which needed to be complete, but can also look forward to the more inclusive promises of the messianic age, described by Micah (4.1–4) and Isa. (2.1–4), when 'nation shall not lift up sword against nation, neither shall they learn war any more'.

150 A symphony of praise

The Psalter ends with this magnificent hymn of praise which has been described 'as the grandest symphony of praise to God ever composed on earth'. To stand in St Paul's Cathedral at the Sung Eucharist, as I did Sunday by Sunday for two years, and to hear the great choir, accompanied by a famous organist on one of the finest organs, lifts the heart to heaven and makes it overflow with tears of worship and ecstasy.

The call to praise God in his sanctuary, is not the Temple in Jerusalem nor a cathedral in Britain, but the Temple of his holiness in heaven itself. The whole of mankind is called to praise him for his mighty acts in human history and for his eternal greatness.

This culminating psalm lists some of the musical instruments used in temple worship – the *shofar* or ram's horn sounded by the priests, the sweet psaltery and harp, the cymbals both loud and more tuneful, strings and pipe – all blend in a torrent of praise, ending with the call

LET EVERYTHING THAT HATH BREATH PRAISE THE LORD! HALLELUJAH!

Jesus and the Psalms

Jesus was born, lived and died a Jew. He attended the synagogue on the sabbath, often preached in the synagogues of Galilee and in the Temple courts at Jerusalem, he kept the great festivals when psalms of praise and thanksgiving would be sung. He would be familiar with the psalms.

He had frequently told his disciples 'that everything written about me in the law of Moses and the prophets and the psalms must be fulfilled', and in the first meeting in his risen form with the eleven disciples he reminded them of this (Luke 24.44). Luke adds, 'Then he opened their minds to understand the scriptures' (Luke 24.44–45).

In controversial discussion with the Pharisees a few days before the crucifixion, Jesus quotes psalm 110.1. 'The Lord said to my Lord, Sit at my right hand till I put thy enemies under thy feet' (Mark 12.36, followed by Matt. 22.44 and Luke 20.42). The writer of the Epistle to the Hebrews notes from the same psalm, 'Thou art a priest for ever after the order of Melchizedek', and interprets it of Christ, as a high priest for all mankind (6.20, 7.17, 21–22).

Psalm 2.6, 'I will announce the Lord's decree that which He has spoken, "You are my son this day have I begotten you"'. Some Christians relate this to the baptism of Jesus, others to Rom. 1.4 where Paul speaks of Jesus 'designated son of God in power according to the spirit of holiness by his resurrection from the dead'.

Psalm 22 most clearly relates to Jesus in the gospels.

171

Mark supported by Matthew records, 'And when the sixth hour had come, there was darkness over the whole land until the ninth hour. And at the ninth hour Jesus cried with a loud voice, 'Eloi, Eloi lama sabachthani?' That cry is the first verse of psalm 22.

It may well have been that on that first Good Friday, the *Khamsin*, the hot wind from the desert was blowing during that three hours, with the air full of sand, like a thick fog, making it difficult to see clearly. (This actually happened on one of the days in my first Holy Week in Jerusalem.)

It could have been that there was darkness also in the soul of Jesus during that time, and that a feeling of loneliness enveloped him, when even God seemed hidden. There came into his memory the first verse of psalm 22, the cry of an earlier sufferer which somehow expressed his own feeling of desolation. Even so, both with the psalmist and with Jesus it was a cry of magnificent faith: '*My* God! *My* God! Why? Why?', yet still '*My* God!'

It would, however, seem to me more likely that Jesus was meditating on the whole psalm, with its alternating rhythm of pain and faith, and its magnificent conclusion of faith and praise in verses 23–32. As I think of him hanging there on the cross, physically exhausted, with death drawing near, yet looking to the future beyond death, trusting that God in his providence and wisdom would make known to future generations the meaning of it all, when the ends of the earth would remember and turn to the Lord, and all the nations would come to worship him, when people yet unborn would learn of the love and forgiveness revealed in the Cross, and countless souls would declare in heartfelt devotion, I cannot escape the conviction, 'This is indeed the Saviour of the world!'

A moment after the cry of desolation from psalm 22,

the dying Jesus remembers a further verse from the psalms to express the last thought in his incarnate life, and his unfailing trust in eternal love and life: 'Father, into your hands I commit my spirit', in a loud voice so that many watching could hear: 'And having said this', says Luke, 'he breathed his last'. The Christian standing in imagination, with the little sad group at the foot of the cross, may wonder if the second part of the verse remembered may also have been in our Lord's mind: 'Thou hast redeemed me, O Lord, faithful God' (Luke 23.46, Psa. 31.5).

Some Early Christian Psalms

Most of the earliest Christians would have been Jews, familiar with the psalms sung in the Temple and synagogues. It would seem probable that among them might be a poet who would add to the traditional collection of psalms some to celebrate their faith that Jesus was the Messiah. It is interesting that a number of such songs was included by Luke the gentile, in his gospel. He may have discovered them in the careful enquiries of which he speaks in the prologue to his gospel (1.1–4). Or he may have heard Christians talk of their memories of the mother of Jesus, the father of John the Baptist, and others connected with the birth of Christ. He may even have met the holy Mother herself and heard from her own lips what we Christians speak of as the wondrous birth, and then worked them into songs which Christians recite almost every day.

Such psalms we now call canticles. They include the *Magnificat*, the *Benedictus*, the *Gloria in Excelsis* of the angels, the *Nunc Dimittis* of the aged priest Simeon, who took the babe Jesus into his arms when he was presented to God in the Temple.

Christians later added, as canticles, psalms from the Book of Psalms, notably psalm 95, the *Venite* as we call it, an invitation to join in morning worship; psalm 100 calling to all lands to be joyful in God our creator and shepherd; psalm 67 praying that God will bless all nations; the *Benedicite* or Song of the Three Children saved from a fiery furnace and later the magnificent psalm of praise associated in tradition with Saints

174

Ambrose and Augustine which we call *Te Deum Laudamus*. At the conclusion of every psalm sung, Christians added a gloria of their own, praising God in his three-fold unity of being, salvation and sanctification.

Other passages in the New Testament are thought to have been used in worship in the age of the apostles. These include what is called the Easter Anthem stringing together three sayings of Paul in praise of the Resurrection (1 Cor. 5.7, Rom. 6.9, 1 Cor. 15.20). Also included is Rev. 4.11 with 5.9—10 entitled 'Glory and Honour', Rev. 15.3—4 headed 'Great and Wonderful', and a little mosaic of thoughts and texts beginning 'Jesus, Saviour of the World'.

The highest peak of faith is seen by many in what is called 'The Song of Christ's Glory', Paul's credal tribute to Jesus in Phil. 2.6—11.

Paul exhorted the Christians in Ephesus to 'address one another in songs and hymns and spiritual songs, singing and making melody to the Lord with all your heart' (5.19). Even the austere and reticent James, spoken of as 'the brother of the Lord', adds his instruction, 'Is any cheerful? Let him sing praise' (5.13). So, many voices from the past urge those of us in each present to follow psalmists, poets and singers in praise of God.

The Psalter opened with psalms going back to David, and ended with the great symphony of praise 'Let everything that hath breath, praise the Lord'. This short survey of the beginning of Christian psalmody reaches its peak of praise in three texts from the book of Revelation:

The kingdoms of this world are become the kingdoms of our Lord, and of his Christ; and He shall reign for ever and ever (11.15). For the Lord God

175

omnipotent reigneth King of Kings and Lord of lords (19.6 and 16).

The selection and juxtaposition of these three texts was an insight of spiritual genius, magnified and immortalized by Handel in a symphony of praise which we call 'The Hallelujah Chorus'.

Verses to Remember

For with Thee is the well of life: and in thy light shall we see light (36.9)

In the hour of my fear: I will put my trust in you (56.3)

As a deer longs for the running brooks: so longs my soul for you, O God. (42.1)

My soul is thirsty for God, thirsty for the living God: when shall I come and see his face (42.2)

I love you, O Lord my strength: O Lord my crag, my fortress and my deliverer. (18.1)

I have said to the Lord you are my Lord: and all my good depends on you. (16.2)

Leave it all quietly to God, my soul, my rescue comes from him alone; rock, rescue, refuge, He is all to me (62.1–2 Moffatt).

You light my lamp O Lord my God: You make my darkness to be bright. (18.30)

Whom have I in heaven but you? and there is no one upon earth that I desire in comparison with you. (73.25)

The Lord is my light and my salvation, whom then shall I fear? The Lord is the stronghold of my life, of whom shall I be afraid? (27.1)

All my fresh springs shall be in thee (87.7b. BCP version)

Heaviness may endure for a night, but joy comes in the morning. (30.5b)

Be still and know that I am God (46.10)

Blessed is the man whose strength is in you ... who going through the valley of dryness finds there a spring from which to drink. (84.5−6)

Today if only you would hear his voice! (95.8)

He will not fear bad tidings: his heart is steadfast, trusting in the Lord (112.7).

I have gone astray like a sheep that is lost: O seek your servant (119.176)

I wait for the Lord, my soul waits for him: and in his word is my hope (130.5)

Praise the Lord O my soul: while I live will I praise the Lord; while I have any being: I will sing praises to my God (146.1−2)

Let everything that has breath praise the Lord (150.6)

Index of Themes